T0064106

THE NARROW WAY

THE NARROW WAY

A COMMON MAN'S ROADMAP TO DIVINITY

PITCHARAN

PARTRIDGE
A Penguin Random House Company

NIHIL OBSTAT: Msgr. Dr. M. Soosai,
Vicar-General of Dharmapuri,
Tamil Nadu.

IMPRIMATUR: Most Rev. Dr. Lawrence Pius Dorairaj, DD
Bishop of Dharmapuri,
Tamil Nadu.

ISBN: Softcover   978-1-4828-4756-7
             eBook   978-1-4828-4755-0

Print information available on the last page.

To order additional copies of this book, contact
Partridge India
000 800 10062 62
orders.india@partridgepublishing.com

www.partridgepublishing.com/india

- An excerpt from the diary of Blessed Mother Teresa, siouxlander. blogspot.in/2012/10/reading-mother-teresa.html
- *Against Julian* (*Contra Julianum*), St. Augustine of Hippo, translated by Matthew A. Schumacher, CSC. Fathers of the Church, Inc., New York, 1957, archive.org

Contents

10. Aids to divinity-III: Suffering

11. The Divine Virtues

12. Keeping Satan at bay

13. The perfect way of our Triune God

14. Conclusion

Appendix: The Way of the Cross

ABBREVIATIONS USED

Catechism of the Catholic Church	CCC	New American Standard Bible	NASB
Corinthians	Cor	New International Version	NIV
Deuteronomy	Deu	New Testament	NT
Douay-Rheims Bible	DRB	Old Testament	OT
Exodus	Ex	Philippians	Php
Ezekiel	Ezk	Proverbs	Pro
Galatians	Gal	Psalms	Ps
Genesis	Gen	Revelation	Rev
Hebrews	Heb	Romans	Rom
Isaiah	Is	Samuel	Sam
Jeremiah	Jer	The Imitation of Christ	IoC
John	Jn	The Jerusalem Bible	JB
Leviticus	Lev	The Sinner's Guide	SG
Luke	Lk	The World English Bible	WEB
Malachi	Mal	Thessalonians	Thes
Mark	Mk	Timothy	Tim
Matthew	Mt	Zechariah	Zech

FOREWORD

To savour the sweetness of contemplation, one has to accept the bitter dryness and aridity in prayer. Jesus' call to his disciples was to follow him on the "narrow way". This book is a manual for persons who are desirous of progressing in the path of holiness. The author beautifully depicts the path of purification of self from the disorderly attachment, as the sure way of genuine freedom and attachment to God. St. John of the Cross has this beautiful saying that a bird is not free to fly if it is tied even by a small rope. Similarly, even the venial attachments our soul cherishes to transitory things, enslaves it from liberating itself and attaching to God. Pitcharan's book is a big help for people to be spiritually motivated and to progress constantly, till one attains the final goal of union with God.

Pitcharan sketches before us the narrow way of spiritual life which is very much linked with the sacramental life of the Church. He beautifully fits in the different sacraments – particularly that of Reconciliation and Eucharist, as sacraments that nurture regularly our spiritual growth. The author quotes many of the well-known spiritual authors and writings to substantiate his point that the narrow way in some manner consists in accepting and enduring the sufferings of this life and the joyful acceptance of the hardships of this life is the anticipation of the Purgatory afterlife (Appendix, ch. 2).

From the wisdom of the Fathers of the Church we come to know the difference between a sinner and a saint. The margin is very narrow but very difficult to cross. Both sinners and saints are invited to the divine furnace of love, which is God. The sinner approaches this burning furnace and feels its heat and says that it is too much and steps back; while the saint approaches the divine furnace and being attracted by the fire of love, throws oneself into it to be consumed by the divine love. The beautiful imagery used by St. John of the Cross for the perfect purification is that of a piece of log that is thrown into the fire. If the log is still moist and not fully dry, it produces a lot of noise, smoke and disturbance. But after a while when the fire expels the moisture, the log starts to burn quietly and gradually it is transformed into burning coal. Pitcharan presents in his book different impurities in us that can disturb the harmony of true contemplation of God, just like the moisture in the log of wood. The harmony of life is attained when our will blends with the divine will in the total surrender of self to God, which he describes as self-annihilation or kenosis (Ch. 7).

The culmination of the author's reflection on the Narrow Way is found in the personalized reflection on the Way of the Cross as the Appendix of this work. This existential reflection on the traditional Way of the Cross is a way of living the Narrow Way in our day to day life. I am happy to present this book to all the readers and seekers of God who are desirous of progressing in the path of holiness.

– Fr. Jose Kumblolickal msfs

Bangalore,
25th March, 2015.

(**Rev. Dr. Jose Kumblolickal msfs,** is the Provincial Superior, South West India Province of the Missionaries of St. Francis de Sales & Vice-Chairman, Indian Institute of Spirituality, Bangalore.)

PREFACE

In spite of our shortcomings, weaknesses and offensive tendencies, most of us fear God and often demonstrate our love and reverence for Him. This however is changing and we also see many who are critical of the very idea of God and even more critical of those who believe in God while there are many others totally unconcerned and least interested in God. Irrespective of which group we belong to, our destinations are the same—ultimate union with God. It is He who always calls the shots and we never know when He is going to surprise whom or how He selects them.

After an unexpected and unusual encounter, I felt the same urge as Andrew after he had met Jesus: *The first thing Andrew did was to find his brother Simon and tell him, "We have found the Messiah"* (NIV Jn 1:41). This urge did not end with just talking to many but grew into a persistent yearning to share all what I learnt about how to attain that common goal of every human soul.

We come across several teachings like this: *Try, then, to imitate God, as children of his that he loves, and follow Christ by loving as he loved you.* (JB Eph 5:1,2a) They tell us clearly 'what', but we are invariably at a loss when it comes to 'how'.

- Do I know the way?
- Is it revealed or described anywhere?
- Am I clear about it or am I still searching for the way?
- Have I not panicked many a time and either considered or consulted astrologers?

- Have I not been drawn to many tricksters who claimed to know the way to God?
- Does God talk to me? How do I appear in God's view?
- Is there a link between how God sees me and the troubles or joys that I encounter?
- Am I struggling to walk the way? Am I still in doubt, though believing?
- Have I understood Church teachings and accepted them with clarity and conviction?
- Do I find it convenient to simply hear and believe the Word without bothering to live it?
- Have I attended a charismatic retreat, only to find that God touched many but left me untouched?

Questions such as above often bombarded me. True, my struggles and efforts to find answers were not in vain, but more and more difficult questions kept coming, like this one: How do I love a brutally perverse rapist who dismembers and destroys a fellow human and shatters the victim's loved ones and terrifies society?

Gradually I came to understand and believe that we are all on an apparently unending journey of learning and transforming during which we are initially torn between godliness and worldliness and finally opt for one of these **three ways**:

a) reject godliness for worldliness and turn degenerate
b) pretend to pursue godliness outwardly but remain worldly deep within and live as successful hypocrites
c) decide firmly one fine day and start pursuing godliness seriously, and then
   o face admiration, get puffed up, stumble, rise again and learn that there is lots more to learn

o   feel elated often and also become downcast sooner or later, but invariably bounce back every time by grace
o   learn from teachings, inspirations, troubles and joys
o   shed proud curiosity and only seek answers with genuine quest
o   become unpopular and face persecution for the love of truth
o   continually avail divine aid to amend self and transform, unmindful of both admiration and insult

The first two options are the **wide ways** to destruction which attract many; the third option is **the narrow way** with few takers which is what this book is all about. The motive is to describe in contemporary common man's language, how we may cooperate with God to be made fit by Him to indwell in His eternal abode.

Towards this, I have tried to put together all my learnings, inspired thoughts and ideas and compile a common man's perception of divinity and the way to attain it. In the process, I have borrowed heavily from my previous work —AGAPE: THE DIVINIZING LOVE, restructuring it and rendering ideas taken from it in common man's language, as well as I could.

To provide an apt imagery of **the narrow way**, a dialogue form of meditation on the traditional **Stations of the Cross**, is excerpted from my previous work and included as an APPENDIX.

I gratefully place on record, the loving encouragement and guidance of my Bishop, His Grace the Most Rev. Dr. Lawrence Pius, which I have been enjoying ever since I took to writing.

I acknowledge with deep gratitude, the magnanimity and kindness of the renowned *spiritual theologian*, Rev. Dr. Jose Kumblolickal, who readily acceded to my request to write the Foreword, even though he did not know me before.

I sincerely thank my colleagues in Christ — Mr. Guilherme Vaz, Dr. John Dayal and Dr. Mary Regina, for sparing precious time to read my manuscript and giving their views.

- Pitcharan

Hosur,
25th March, 2015.

~ 1 ~

INTRODUCTION

In Matthew 5, Lord Jesus describes righteous requirements which are radical and path-breaking in several ways. They exceedingly surpass what was considered as sufficient for salvation, by the scribes and teachers of divine law of those times:

- He equates anger with murder and lustful looks with adultery
- He brands the legalization of remarriage after divorce, as a disguised form of adultery that was institutionalized by hard-hearted men
- He rejects the belief that marriage is a mere contract between humans and declares it an indissoluble sacrament instituted by God
- He exhorts humans to become perfect like their heavenly Father, loving and blessing enemies rather than hating and cursing them.

The righteous requirements to be fulfilled for becoming fit children of God constitute the 'what'. The challenge lies in deciphering the 'how' and defining a practical roadmap comprising aids and pitfalls in the salvation journey. While there is no dearth of 'what' (dos and don'ts) there is very little on 'how' and it seems to have always been that way. A few examples from salvation history are given below to highlight the problem:

- Our first parents were told by God what to do and what not to do and yet they stumbled because they did not bother how.
- The Law was revealed through Moses and the Israelites learnt it by heart – what to do and what not to do; yet, most of them stumbled because they did not care to know how to fulfill the Law.
- *"You diligently study the Scriptures because you think that by them you possess eternal life. These are the Scriptures that testify about me, yet you refuse to come to me to have life"*. (NIV Jn 5:39-40)
- *"For I have the desire to do what is good, but I cannot carry it out."* (NIV Rom 7:18cd)

To get it even clearer, consider this important 'what', viz., 'believing in the Lord'. We have learnt that the believer is aided by divine grace and gradually transformed. Have we learnt how to believe? The 'how' for the most important 'what' is certainly there to be deciphered, otherwise our Lord would not have commanded us to believe. This is true for all of God's commands.

One day I found the 'secret of life' (जीवन का राज़) revealed crisply but most profoundly in this couplet by the very renowned saint-poet—Thiruvalluvar, whose religious affiliation remains a mystery till this day amidst conflicting claims:

பிறவிப்பெருங்கடல் நீந்துவர்; நீந்தார்
இறைவன் அடி சேராதார். (Kural 10)

The meaning that came so clearly to my mind differed completely from all known and popular interpretations. It hit me like a great revelation, initially confounding only to turn most convincing: *We are born to struggle and life on earth is like an ocean which we must swim across; those who refuse to swim (struggle) are the ones who fail to reach God.*

I further realized, that becoming fully fit may seem impossible while on earth, but our shortcomings cannot declare us as evil. All that we must do is keep struggling without giving up and reminds me of what Jesus Himself had said or implied more than once: *"But he that shall persevere unto the end, he shall be saved".* (DRB Mt 10:22 or Mt 24:13 or Mk 13:13).

While universities use the term 'divinity' synonymously with 'theology', it means different things to different people and some of the most common definitions or descriptions include: Godlike nature, holiness, righteousness, goodness, saintliness, humanism, etc. But it is best understood as **ultimate fitness to live with God in heaven**.

Our destination is God and for all those who realize this fundamental truth, life on earth becomes most meaningful. It is influenced and directed by an inherent inclination for doing good and an aversion for evil. These in turn are driven by a strong desire to find a dwelling place in His eternal abode in the afterlife which builds the faithful day by day, even providing strength to endure every trouble for the sake of attaining this ultimate goal.

An experiential view of **the narrow way** in a nut-shell or simply 'the journey of life' as envisioned by a common man like me, is excerpted from my previous work and reproduced below:

A strange encounter changed my heart
And spurred me on to seek Him oft.
Hitherto in darkness dwelling
I was gifted understanding.

Peace and pain took regular turns
Taming volatility that burns.
All of that and even more
Prepared me for every throe.
My yearning every moment grew
I felt the change they call 'renew'.
Me never did it ever strike
What the narrow way looked like.

That Lent is unforgettable
When I was found eligible
To know about the road ahead,
And say YES rather than dread.

The journey that I'd embarked on
Like a well lit passage shone.
The Way to God now became clear;
Wonder how I shed my fear.

~ 2 ~

GOING ASTRAY
THE UNGRATEFUL WAY

When they came into Paradise, Adam and Eve were without blemish and lacked nothing; they were God's children who were in direct touch with Him. Similarly, the Israelites of Exodus were also showered with innumerable bounties: freedom from cruel slavery, water-manna-quails in the desert and were led by God's handpicked prophet —Moses, who spoke face to face with God on their behalf. But then what happened very soon in both cases?

"They have acted perversely, those he begot without blemish" (JB Deu 32:5a).

He banished the man, and in front of the garden of Eden he posted the cherubs, and the flame of a flashing sword, to guard the way to the tree of life (JB Gen 3:24).

Consider Adam and Eve; how did they fall into sin? How could Eve blindly reject her maker's warning and readily believe the deceiver's lie? How could Adam follow suit so meekly? If this happened with them, how are we better off? What is our security against temptation?

Solving this puzzle is our first and foremost priority and unless we understand how, we too are bound to lose the way just like our first parents and the Israelites of Exodus: *"They have been quick to leave the way I marked out for them".* (JB Ex 32:8a)

Repeated reading of the Genesis account (chapters 2 & 3) and much pondering, led me to logically deduce the following:

- God provided Adam and Eve with everything and they lacked nothing
- God forewarned them about the consequences of eating the forbidden fruit
- Satan was able to deceive them into buying his lie and rejecting the truth
- Since Satan could do this, Adam and Eve were obviously vulnerable
- If they were vulnerable then they really lacked something
- But God had provided them everything; so what did they lack?
- Which means, whatever they lacked was not something from God
- It must have certainly been something within their own capacity and control
- What was it? The only thing that I could think of is this — gratitude.

Logic is fine, but can we really conclude that the fall was caused by ingratitude? Maybe yes, as it is exactly what this tall saint believed, that he even wrote: *Ingratitude is the most abominable of sins and as such it is the cause, beginning, and origin of all sins and misfortunes.* (St. Ignatius of Loyola in his letter to Father Simão Rodrigues —18 Mar 1542).

Adam and Eve had no sense of gratitude for all the goodies they received from God. If only there had been in them even a slight sense of gratitude, it would have gained them grace to hold fast to God's command and reject Satan's apparently attractive offer. The saving grace would have enabled seeing through Satan's deception; sadly that was not to be. They ungratefully failed to provide any place for God in their hearts, rendering themselves vulnerable and paving the way for Satan to inject pride.

They became spiritually blind because of their pride and stooped so low to do these detestable deeds:

- Eve took Satan's advice to become like God.
- Adam followed suit and later went on to literally blame God by responding: *"The woman you put here with me"* (NIV Gen 3:12b).

Had Eve truly been in awe of God she would have rather told Him plainly: "Lord I am in awe of You; teach me Your ways". It is quite obvious, that she had become filled with pride and envy after listening to Satan and Adam's behaviour is the height of pride; Eve blamed the serpent but Adam blamed God.

In the words of St. Augustine of Hippo: *For, if the human senses had not then received the 'root of evil', there would not have been assent to the evil persuasion.* (Against Julian, I, 9.42; page 50). Disobedience, 'carnal cravings' and many other such sinful natures (vices) are all the offspring of pride.

Never suffer pride to reign in your mind or in your words, for from it all perdition took its beginning. (DRB Tobit 4:14)

When we fail to respond with gratitude for all of God's bounties, we are only inviting Satan to afflict us with pride which will render us spiritually blind and slaves to all kind of sinful natures. **Pride** blinds spiritual vision and opens the 'eyes of inability'. Such a person turns hard-hearted. **Hardness of heart** can be best described as **unbelief caused by spiritual blindness that rejects truth despite glaring solid evidence but readily accepts untruth without any proof.**

"He said to him, 'If they do not listen to Moses and the Prophets, they will not be convinced even if someone rises from the dead.'" (NIV Lk 16:31)

"... when your fathers put me to the test; when they tried me, though they saw my work." (Ps 95:9)

They fashioned a calf at Horeb and worshipped an image of metal, exchanging the God who was their glory to the image of a bull that eats grass. They forgot the God who was their saviour, who had done such great things in Egypt, such portents in the land of Ham, such marvels at the Red Sea. (Ps 106:19-22)

We can see that **disobedience** is the original sin and the cause is **pride** which entered humans because of **ingratitude**. Remember the Israelites in the Desert of Sin, who were ungrateful for the innumerable bounties received. It is because of their ingratitude that they had no abiding grace to fulfill God's Law and stumbled badly.

For although they knew God, they neither glorified Him as God nor gave thanks to Him, but their thinking became futile and their foolish hearts were darkened. (NIV Rom 1:21)

~ 3 ~

HOW FREE IS OUR
FREE WILL?

We bear the image and likeness of God and are trinitarian beings just like Him. By virtue of this structure, **our spirit counsels**, **our mind wills i.e., decides**, and **our heart does (executes) the will** (explained elaborately in chapter 13). All our actions follow from the decisive choices we make between good and evil. We are given a spirit that guides us to choose what is good but our defiled heart is prone to do what is evil, manipulated by the senses. *"The spirit is willing, but the body* (heart) *is weak"* (NIV Mt 26:41b).

Thus, one may succumb to the palate's craving and choose to be a glutton only to suffer stomach upsets, but still refuse to listen to the spirit that says, "Enough, stop eating!" Again, one may ignore conscience and despise one's own father, driven by the heart's pride.

These **wrong choices are sins** and could be thoughts, words, actions or inactions and the defilement that drives us to commit them is **vice** or **sinfulness**. This is the process of falling into sin—once we allow pride to gain entry into our hearts we become interiorly defiled. This defilement causes us to suffer from sinful urge and we are helpless against temptations and despite desiring good end up sinning against our own will.

"I have been sold as a slave to sin. I cannot understand my own behavior. I fail to carry out the things I want to do, and I find myself doing the very things I hate. When I act against my own will, that means I have a self that acknowledges that the Law is good, and so the thing behaving in that way is not my self but sin living in me" (JB Rom 7:14b-17).

Pride is our Enemy Number One that puts us in constant conflict with God, neighbour and self. The ones who are afflicted by pride tend to be: carnal, weak, easily hurt, envious, curious, nosey, covetous, unhappy, fearful, volatile, quarrelsome, fault-finding, self-righteous, intolerant, impatient, irritable, bitter, moody, unforgiving, negative and in the worst cases: crazy, schizophrenic or suicidal.

Just as it takes two hands to produce a clap, it takes two forces to commit a sin. An **external temptation** pulls us while an **internal sinful urge** pushes us and we fall into the quagmire called sin.

Pride has inflicted these twin damages on our beings: our minds have been rendered confused and wavering while our hearts have become corrupt. The corrupted heart craves for sensual pleasures. The wavering mind is torn between our spirit and our heart, and Satan is able to manipulate our heart through the senses. Thus, the spirit's good counsel is more often than not, overruled by the carnal craving of the heart.

Knowing about the perils of carnal pleasures is not sufficient as we are already under the power of sin and it is impossible to break-free on our own. How do I benefit from knowledge? *For I have the desire to do what is good, but I cannot carry it out* (NIV Rom 7:18cd).

Our free will is no longer free, as the decision of the mind, though based on truth supplied by our spirit, is often overruled by our corrupted heart. A wavering mind, that allows a disobedient heart to do its whim rather than the true will, is nothing short of slavery to evil.

~ 4 ~

TRUE FREEDOM

Once we realize that the senses rob us of our freedom and often steer our heart against our will, we search for a way out and try hard to assert our control over our senses. What we find and choose to follow is, either the foolish way:

- forcibly suppress the sensual appetite, blindly observe the Law only in letter and turn into a 'holier than thou' self-righteous self-made saint who looks down on many as shameless sinners

or the wise way:

- sincerely accept the Law as good and strive to abide; after much stumbling surrender helplessly to God pleading for mercy.

Trying to overcome the flesh by sheer human effort is folly and suppressing the sensual appetite is **foolish puritanism**. One may ask: What is so foolish about being puritanical? The folly lies in the fact that suppression of sensual appetite will only make it manifest in undesirable ways or erupt like a volcano one day.

Unreasonably implementing the Law is **fanatical fundamentalism**. Here is an example of this horrible folly in action: *Going on from that place, he went into their synagogue, and a man with a shrivelled hand was there. Looking for a reason to accuse Jesus, they asked him,* **"Is it lawful to heal on the Sabbath?"** *He said to them, "If any of you has a sheep and it falls into a pit on the Sabbath, will you not take hold of it and lift it out? How much more valuable is a man than a sheep! Therefore it is lawful to do good on the Sabbath." Then he said to the man, "Stretch out your hand." So he stretched it out and it was completely restored, just as sound as the other.* **But the Pharisees went out and plotted how they might kill Jesus.** (NIV Mt 12:9-14)

The Parable of the Ten Virgins, provides an excellent imagery of the imminent end that awaits the over confident foolish and the vigilant wise. Virginity symbolises fidelity in terms of single-minded or undivided focus in seeking God's kingdom. As we do not know when we will have to face judgment, we need to be most vigilant and maintain a worthy state always. This humanly impossible task turns possible for those who surrender to God.

"At that time the kingdom of heaven will be like ten virgins who took their lamps and went out to meet the bridegroom. Five of them were foolish and five were wise. The foolish ones took their lamps but did not take any oil with them. The wise, however, took oil in jars along with their lamps. The bridegroom was a long time in coming, and they all became drowsy and fell asleep. "At midnight the cry rang out: 'Here's the bridegroom! Come out to meet him!' "Then all the virgins woke up and trimmed their lamps. The foolish ones said to the wise, 'Give us some of your oil; our lamps are going out.' "'No,' they replied, 'there may not be enough for both us and you. Instead, go to those who sell oil and buy some for yourselves.' "But while they were on their way to buy the oil, the bridegroom arrived. The virgins who were ready

*went in with him to the wedding banquet. And the door was shut.
"Later the others also came. 'Sir, Sir,' they said, 'Open the door
for us!' "But he replied, 'I tell you the truth, I don't know you.'
"Therefore keep watch, because you do not know the day or the
hour.* (NIV Mt 25:1-13)

The foolish virgins represent the puritanical and fanatical
Pharisees, who thought they were saved by keeping the Law
in letter and neglected the spirit of the Law. The Venerable
Louis of Granada explains the parable thus: *No one makes
intercession with the Bridegroom for the five foolish virgins who,
after despising the pleasures of the flesh and stifling in their hearts
the fire of concupiscence, nay, after observing the great counsel of
virginity, neglected the precept of humility and became inflated
with pride on account of their virginity.* (SG-8)

For being reconciled to God, pride which is the **root of evil**
must be shed first, followed by purging of sensual cravings.
Our Lord explains this again most beautifully in the example
of the Pharisee and the tax collector: *The Pharisee stood and
prayed about himself: 'God, I thank you that I am not like
other men—robbers, evildoers, adulterers—or even like this tax
collector. I fast twice a week and give a tenth of all I get.' "But
the tax collector stood at a distance. He would not even look up
to heaven, but beat his breast and said, 'God, have mercy on me,
a sinner.' "I tell you that this man, rather than the other, went
home justified before God. For everyone who exalts himself will
be humbled, and he who humbles himself will be exalted."* (NIV
Lk 18:11-14)

The wise virgins represent humble sinners like the tax
collector who surrendered to God in fear, confessing his utter
helplessness. **Fear of God** is the beginning of wisdom that
slowly but steadily transforms the sinner into a righteous child

of God. The vigil needed to avoid sin and maintain fidelity, is supplied by wisdom that comes from the **fear of God**.

How does fear enable our free will to rule the heart? I felt initially that fear of God leads to surrender and when we surrender, God strengthens our free will which defeats the senses. After some more pondering, my thoughts puzzled me like this: How can surrender give freedom? Why would God expect such a thing? Won't that nullify the very meaning of free will?

Consider Jonah's story; was not his rebellious nature forcibly brought into obedience by God? Why would God force Jonah unless he had already surrendered his free will to God?

After pondering much over this, I understood that the heart can be freed from slavery to the senses only by God's grace, which in turn is gained by surrendering our free will and accepting the most supreme will of God. We go through a great struggle as Satan who all along seduced our heart to disobey our mind now tries a new trick by provoking our mind to assert its freedom and not surrender to God's will. We may overcome this inner struggle by reasoning in our God given mind to clearly deduce that:

- our helplessness against carnal urges is not hopelessness, as it is possible to surrender our free will to God and forfeit the freedom to will and let God be the sovereign Lord who gives us grace
- surrender for gaining grace is not slavery; on the contrary, spirit overcoming the flesh is true freedom and is truly possible with God given grace
- surrendering to God gives true freedom; it is strange but true

- *Whoever tries to keep his life will lose it, and whoever loses his life will preserve it* (NIV Lk 17:33).
- Grace is the Divine Power that enables aligning free will to the ever prevailing God's Will and is freely given to those who surrender to Him
- Those who surrender thus are the elect who are taunted most by Satan to reclaim their surrendered free will
- **The surrendered elect** can be clearly recognized in the lives of many: Mother Mary, Lord Jesus, Apostle Paul, Ignatius of Loyola, Francis of Assisi,...
- **The surrendered elect** do not worry about weaknesses if any: *Therefore I will boast all the more gladly about my weaknesses.* (NIV 2Cor 12:9d)
- Freedom from vices if any and growing to perfection in virtues is accomplished in them by grace: *"My grace is sufficient for you, for my power is made perfect in weakness".* (NIV 2Cor 12:9bc)
- **Heaven is a matter of firm choice made by a free will that does not lose its freedom to sensuality or adversity but remains steadfast to the end against all odds**.
- False freedom does what is pleasing to the senses, only to regret after it is too late; true freedom obeys God without minding troubles, only to reap eternal joy in the end.
- Surrendering free will to God is actually like placing it in God's loving care because of our helplessness in preserving its true freedom.
- *Do not possess anything that can hinder you or rob you of freedom. Be resigned to My will and you will suffer no loss.* (IoC III:27)

God does not take away freedom but enables us to preserve it even as the going gets tougher. Recall **the Agony in the Garden of Gethsemane** when our Lord remained steadfast in adversity: *"Father, if you are willing, take this cup from me; yet not my will, but yours be done"* (NIV Lk 22:42).

~ 5 ~

FINDING THE NARROW WAY

God's compassion came to mankind's rescue in their miserable state after the fall—*The Lord God made garments of skin for Adam and his wife and clothed them.* (NIV Gen 3: 21). We also learn that it is God's loving nature to, not only rescue the injured and fallen, but also warn those heading for a fall. Did He not forewarn Cain lovingly? *"But if you do not do what is right, sin is crouching at your door; it desires to have you, but you must master it."* (NIV Gen 4: 7bcd).

When we fail to heed His warnings or proudly spurn His loving overtures, God affords us the luxury of falling which is a blessing in disguise, precisely meant to bring us to our senses. The Parable of the Prodigal Son provides the most beautiful imagery of God's saving love: *He longed to fill his stomach with the pods that the pigs were eating, but no one gave him anything. When he **came to his senses**, he said, 'How many of my father's hired men have food to spare, and here I am starving to death! I will set out and go back to my father and say to him: Father, I have sinned against heaven and against you. I am no longer worthy to be called your son; make me like one of your hired men.' So he got up and went to his father. But while he was still a long way off, his father saw him and was filled with compassion for him; he ran to his son, threw his arms around him and kissed him.* (NIV Lk 15:16-20)

In this parable, our Lord implicitly but profoundly reveals this—**suffering brings us to our senses so that we may undergo a change of heart**. Our pride can be shed only when we come to our senses after the fall which invariably follows pride. God humbles the proud hearted only to save them and not to humiliate them; shedding pride after a fall is a wonderfully joyful experience. **Every time we suffer a setback or major disappointment or failure despite best efforts, it is an opportunity and Godsend invite to enter the narrow way**.

Slavery to sin distances a person from God and has the natural consequence of restlessness and a craving for rest and peace. At a chosen time, God confronts the sinner with the offer to liberate. This is the time of reckoning and the greatest opportunity. A sinner's acceptance of God's offer begins with **change of heart** (*metanoia*). The humbling induced change of heart, places a person on the road to divinity which is the narrow way. It is literally crossing over from death to life; recall what our Lord taught: *"I tell you the truth, whoever hears my word and believes him who sent me has eternal life and will not be condemned; he has crossed over from death to life"* (NIV John 5:24).

God woos all kinds of sinners to conversion and designs a unique situation for each person to come to his / her senses and avail a free and fair chance to choose between the narrow way to divinity and the wide ways to destruction. Even if we fail to realize and respond, God never gives up on us. We are allowed to test the consequence of our choices and for our wrong moves, given the longest rope of chances to learn and change course. Pharaoh was given eleven chances to let the Israelites go free (read Exodus 7-11; here 'eleven' is used symbolically to convey the same meaning as in the English idiom 'eleventh hour').

David was able to weep and repent for his heinous crime as he readily received the grace which was offered in an extra special manner by God through Nathan (see 2Sam 12). God may bend backwards to woo sinners to repentance and His strange ways are most effective; but never does He impose grace on anyone forcibly. Judas Iscariot spurned all offers of this grace and finally when he was overwhelmed by remorse he failed to repent and ended up hanging himself. We must also read other examples of conversion like those of Saul the Pharisee (see Acts 9) and the Jailer of Philippi (see Acts 16).

A rather difficult parable is that of the Dishonest Steward (see Lk 16) which stands out as the most stunning example of how God woos the corrupt and dishonest to conversion, while the self-righteous remain unmoved. When Jesus narrated this parable He targeted two groups of people: one that was despised and frowned upon by society and another that enjoyed much honour and respect. Both shared this common love—amassing wealth. The openly corrupt taxmen are referred to as 'children of this world'; the Pharisees who fanatically kept the Law, believing it to be the 'Light of Life', are described as 'children of light'. The taxmen had no qualms about adopting dishonest means but were known for their liberal spending habits and for using ill-gotten wealth freely to gain favors and friends. The Pharisees amassed wealth through legally right ways but were known to be tightfisted with their hard-earned money. The former are commended for their worldly shrewdness and wooed to give up dishonest ways and receive their own heavenly treasures by proving trustworthy with what belongs to others. The latter are commended for their honesty and advised to freely use money to gain the friendship of saints who would welcome them into 'eternal dwellings', when their legalistic righteousness fails to gain them salvation. Both are candidly told to break free from the love of money and seek God with an undivided heart.

The Pharisees who loved money heard all this and were sneering at Jesus (NIV Lk 16:14). Though there is no mention of how the taxmen responded, we have reasons to believe that the likes of Matthew (also called Levi) and Zacchaeus, were indeed converted by this teaching.

As Jesus went on from there, he saw a man named Matthew sitting at the tax collector's booth. "Follow me," he told him, and Matthew got up and followed him. While Jesus was having dinner at Matthew's house, many tax collectors and "sinners" came and ate with him and his disciples. (NIV Mt 9:9-10)

When Jesus reached the spot, he looked up and said to him, "Zacchaeus, come down immediately. I must stay at your house today!" So he came down at once and welcomed Him gladly. Jesus said to him, "Today salvation has come to this house, because this man, too, is a son of Abraham. For the Son of Man came to seek and to save what was lost." (NIV Lk19:5-6, 9-10).

This is how Jesus won over the corrupt and dishonest taxmen:

- He appreciated the shrewdness of the 'children of this world' in freely spending ill-gotten money on each other but took a mild dig at the honest 'children of light' who were seldom known to liberally spend their hard-earned money, even on their own friends.
- He surprised the taxmen by saying that heavenly treasures belong to them and they will receive that which is their own only if they proved trustworthy with what belongs to others.

- He most effectively exposed the fallacy of trying to love both God and money by drawing a parallel with 'a servant who serves two masters'. In stating this, He acknowledged the fact that, even dishonest and corrupt people love God. But then He clarified most firmly that, undivided Love alone is acceptable to God.

~ 6 ~

ON THE NARROW WAY

The best thing that can ever happen to anyone is 'crossing over from death to life'. However, there is a greater need to consolidate this gain and prevent a reversal and an even greater need to keep moving forward on the narrow way. We must also strive to complete the entire course during our earthly sojourn and leave nothing pending for the afterlife. Only then we would really be imitating our Lord and withstand the divinity test like Him and be able to say *"It is finished"*, before we give up our spirit. Let us then see what it takes to stick to the way, moving forward all the time till we finish the last lap.

STAYING THERE

To break-free from sinning, we need to understand the interior **cause** rather than punish or lament the exterior **effect** (damage). *If your hand causes you to sin, cut it off. And if your foot causes you to sin, cut it off. And if your eye causes you to sin, pluck it out* (NIV Mk 9:43a, 45a, 47a). These words are not to be taken in the literal sense; our Lord is merely exhorting us strongly, to target the **cause** of sin rather than direct our efforts entirely against the **effect.**

This is what '**targeting the cause of sin**', is all about:

- reprimanding anger rather than hanging people after their anger culminates in murder;
- deterring lustful looks instead of waiting till it degenerates to adultery and rape;
- preventing crime through education, employment and poverty alleviation
- warning people of the looming perils from human laws that promote foeticide and adultery rather than taking extreme stances that polarize society.

The life and teachings of our Lord and Saviour Jesus enlighten us that love, repentance and forgiveness alone can remit our sins. Sin is a debt that we cannot repay and yet God may cancel the debt of sin for many good reasons: "*Love covers over a multitude of sins. For if you forgive men when they sin against you, your heavenly Father will also forgive you*" (NIV 1Pet 4:8b, Mt 6:14).

Change of heart and repentance are just the beginning and cannot rid us of our sinful tendency in an instant and prevent further sinning. To stop sinning is a long walk to freedom and though humanly impossible, there is sure hope for all those who trust in God. Our helplessness is not hopelessness for our God as we have learnt, is truly the—**help of the helpless** (بے سہاروں کا سہارا) and His power is made perfect in our weaknesses. The battle is truly His and we only have to show our love by refusing to remain slaves but keep struggling. When we suffer humiliation our mind is able to shed pride and come to its senses; when we endure physical pain our heart is able to shed sensual cravings. (Chapter 10 is a detailed treatise on the subject)

Thus, through endured sufferings our spiritual vision is gradually restored and we come to know the truth. Truth sets us free from the bondage to sin and we stop sinning as Satan cannot deceive us like before. *"Then you will know the truth, and the truth will set you free."* (NIV Jn 8:32)

The narrow way is not trouble free and it is vital to know about the fatal pitfalls and steer clearly away from them. *Jesus said to his disciples: "Things that cause people to sin are bound to come, but woe to that person through whom they come. It would be better for him to be thrown into the sea with a millstone tied around his neck than for him to cause one of these little ones to sin. So watch yourselves.* (NIV Lk 17:1-3a). Our Lord is not suggesting an apt punishment for those who lead the innocent to sinning, but forewarning us of the imminent end of such sinners which is worse than being drowned with a millstone round the neck. To put it plain and simple, becoming an extended arm of Satan is the worst degree of degeneration and a fatal sin that maims the ability to undergo a change of heart and repent.

God teaches us to seek Him always through an effective process that resembles the game of 'hide–n–seek'. In this game we are like sunflowers and He is like the Sun; when He covers His face with clouds we become downcast and droop; again as He uncovers His face and shines we light up as our joy returns. He sends periodic bouts of aridity and joy; during these arid moments we feel very dull (not exactly depressed but similar feeling) for no apparent reason and develop a craving for God. They invariably end very soon only to be followed by a bout of joy each time. To endure arid moments praying is best and another practical way is engaging in manual chores like cleaning, arranging and washing; they really soothe the downcast spirit and also help us dwell in humility.

We must NEVER ever conclude that a weakness or vice is dead even after tasting victory that lasts. **At the slightest sign of complacency a vice that was dormant for years may erupt like a volcano and leave you shattered and confused. Virtues too may grow beautifully but a mild self-praising thought is enough to make them shrink or even disappear**. That is why Paul tells us: *"—continue to work out your salvation with fear and trembling"* (NIV Php 2:12d).

However, there is no cause for panic or any need to feel unduly perturbed when it happens as suggested above; **experience alone can teach us** to become absolutely shy of worldly praise which is really vainglory. We will come to understand slowly that as long as we dwell on earth, we may NEITHER give NOR receive praise or glory, except to and from God. Recall what our Lord had said once: *"Why do you call me good?" Jesus answered. "No one is good—except God alone"* (NIV Mk 10:18 or Lk18:19).

David displayed great **faith** when he took on Goliath solely depending on God's strength (see 1Sam 17). But after finding favour with God and winning many battles he behaved like a worldly king who often checks his own strength. He proceeded to take a census of able men for his army only to incur God's wrath for this (see 2Sam 24). God never fails to align the will of His elect: *"Those whom I love I rebuke and discipline"* (NIV Rev 3:19a).

FAST TRACKING

Is it not enough if we stopped sinning? What more should we do to move further and faster on the narrow way? Shedding vices merely enables us to approach God; growing in virtues is the real thing that takes us closer. What are virtues, but good natures; what are vices, but evil natures. We can exchange all our vices for virtues by bearing the Godsend crosses with the help of God supplied grace.

What happens to people who do neither evil nor good and what are good fruits? John the Baptist explains it lucidly: *The ax is already at the root of the trees, and every tree that does not produce good fruit will be cut down and thrown into the fire." "What should we do then?" the crowd asked. John answered, "The man with two tunics should share with him who has none, and the one who has food should do the same"* (NIV Lk 3:9-11).

Our Lord too reinforced the same thing: *Then he told this parable: "A man had a fig tree, planted in his vineyard, and he went to look for fruit on it, but did not find any. So he said to the man who took care of the vineyard, 'For three years now I've been coming to look for fruit on this fig tree and haven't found any. Cut it down! Why should it use up the soil?"* (NIV Lk 13:6-7).

Failure to bear good fruits after being freed from vice implies that we have been ungrateful and are bound to return to our same old sinful state. We must be grateful to God for the taste of freedom from vice and always seek His grace to sustain it and grow in virtue and bear good fruits.

Seeking God's help is our only birthright and we must remember that we are all ***unprofitable servants*** enjoying unmerited privilege to bask in His glory. It is God Who frees us from vice and it is He Who gives us virtue. How can we forget that we belong to Him and that all our power comes from Him? The moment we imagine of things like our own glory, we will fall into the same mire called vice, from which we were rescued by God. Ingratitude brings back pride to our hearts and then we start feeling like chaste Saints. Such thoughts come from Satan whose sole purpose is to separate us

THE NARROW WAY

from God so that we die. *If anyone thinks he is something when he is nothing, he deceives himself* (NIV Gal 6:3).

There is nothing we can do without Him while everything becomes possible if He is with us. His most precious words to be remembered every moment: *"Remain in me, and I will remain in you. No branch can bear fruit by itself; it must remain in the vine. Neither can you bear fruit unless you remain in me. I am the vine; you are the branches. If a man remains in me and I in him, he will bear much fruit; apart from me you can do nothing. If anyone does not remain in me, he is like a branch that is thrown away and withers; such branches are picked up, thrown into the fire and burned"* (NIV Jn 15:4-6).

THE LAST LAP

What happens to a tree which bears fruit only during season? *The next day as they were leaving Bethany, Jesus was hungry. Seeing in the distance a fig tree in leaf, he went to find out if it had any fruit. When he reached it, he found nothing but leaves, because **it was not the season for figs**. Then he said to it, "May you never bear fruit again!" Immediately the tree withered.* (NIV Mk 11:12-13, Mt 21:19cd).

Sharing our surplus with our needy brethren is good but not enough and may be compared to fruits that grow only during season. Denying self to help the needy is the real face of mature love and the beginning of **Agape**. It is the standard that God has set, metaphorically called 'everlasting fruits' that are expected not only during season but at all times. *"This is to my Father's glory, that you bear much fruit, showing yourselves to be my disciples. You did not choose me, but I chose you and appointed you so that you might go and bear fruit—**fruit that will last**"* (NIV Jn 15: 8, 16ab).

We were saved by Him and bore good fruits by His grace. Everlasting fruits too are borne by His grace which is given freely to each of us according to our love and desire for it. Our love is measured in terms of sufferings endured for bearing more fruit; *every branch that does bear fruit He prunes so that it will be even more fruitful* (NIV Jn 15:2b).

The greatest human achievement lies in, loving enslaved brethren, pleading their case with God and joining God in freeing them by enduring suffering and even facing death for this cause. It is accomplished by **Agape** the greatest virtue and dying to save an enemy is the ultimate, as *God demonstrates his own love for us in this: While we were still sinners, Christ died for us* (NIV Rom 5:8).

Fruit trees of all kinds will grow on both banks of the river. Their leaves will not wither, nor will their fruit fail. Every month they will bear fruit, because the water from the sanctuary flows to them. Their fruit will serve for food and their leaves for healing" (NIV Ezk 47:12).

On each side of the river stood the tree of life, bearing twelve crops of fruit, yielding its fruit every month. And the leaves of the tree are for the healing of the nations (NIV Rev 22:2bc).

~ 7 ~

THE PROVING OF DIVINITY

God's supreme sacrifice for the love of humans commences with divesting all glory to be the incarnate 'God with us' and it is just the beginning of **kenosis** or **self-annihilation**.

The fall of humankind was signified by loss of spiritual vision and opening of the 'eyes of inability' as a fallout of which, we see a sibling as a threat and anyone who hurts us as a detestable enemy. Complete restoration of spiritual vision is the first sign of Divinity. Such a person sees a tormentor as a helpless puppet in the hands of principalities (demons) and is also able to foresee the horrible end in store for them and even intercede with compassion. As Jesus approached **total self-annihilation** which is the total emptying of self or **zenith of kenosis**, He who had already demonstrated Divine authority by forgiving sins, chose not to exercise it but humbly pleaded for the forgiveness of his tormentors, like a mere human with full spiritual vision: *Jesus said, "Father, forgive them, for they do not know what they are doing"* (NIV Lk 23:34a). As he was being stoned to death, Stephen foresaw by spiritual vision, where his killers were headed. *Then he fell on his knees and cried out, "Lord, do not hold this sin against them"* (NIV Acts 7:60ab).

The Agony in the Garden of Gethsemane was the extreme pain and anxiety of knowing what was about to happen. It was a prelude to **Baptism by Fire** when God the Father would briefly remain cut-off from the Son. Human language cannot describe the extreme nature of this most painful state when love is not a balm but the cause of pain. But for our Lord's love for the Father, there would have been no pain of being cut-off. True, that love alone can endure all pain; but how does one endure pain when the balm itself is the cause? More love meant more pain and less love was unthinkable. Naturally our Lord's will was forced into a situation of conflict with His Father's will, as it was the most unbearable thing that could ever happen. He remained steadfast in love but did not hide the pain and cried out: *"Father, if you are willing, take this cup from me; yet not my will, but yours be done."* (NIV Lk 22:42)

The ultimate proving of Divinity is through **Baptism by Fire** which is 'being totally cut-off from God briefly'. This test proves that a person loves God purely for God's sake with no other selfish consideration by abiding in love even when cut-off from God. After the prelude at Gethsemane our Lord endured the unimaginable worst pain on the cross when He **completely emptied Himself** even as **He remained totally cut-off from the Father for three hours** and cried out like a human: *"My God! My God! Why have You forsaken me?"* (NIV Mt 27:46c also Mk 15:34c).

For a brief moment I forsook you, But with great compassion I will gather you (NASB Is 54:7). The sign of fully proven Divinity is **beatific vision** which is mystical union with God (refer CCC 1028, 2014 & 2015). After the **Baptism by Fire**, it was with great relief and joy of accomplishment, that *Jesus said, "It is finished." With that, he bowed his head and gave up His spirit* (NIV Jn 19:30bc). The most edifying and **only recorded testimony of the joy that awaits those who endure to the end**, by a disciple who became the first martyr: *But Stephen,* *full of the Holy Spirit, looked up to heaven and saw the glory of God, and Jesus standing at the right hand of God. "Look," he said, "I see heaven open and the Son of Man standing at the right hand of God"* (NIV Acts 7:55-56).

~ 8 ~

AIDS TO DIVINITY-I:
THE CHURCH

The first move that went wrong, earned our original defilement which is a penchant for wrong choice. Salvation is the free gift from God, comprising a complete package of special aids to free us from sinful slavery and endure till the end to reach our predestined goal. *For the wages of sin is death, but the gift of God is eternal life in Christ Jesus our Lord* (NIV Rom 6:23). God came down to earth to save those who were bound to end up as demons in hell by teaching them how to change course and become heaven bound to end up as God's glorious children.

God is making an open offer to all His fallen children, of restoration as sons and daughters through faith in Jesus Christ. The faithful, who avail God's equal opportunity offer, constitute the members of the Church. Thus, the Church is the mystical body of Christ and its faithful members are the abundantly fruitful branches. They are grafted mystically into God's body, and are nourished by the sap of the **Tree of Life**. *So it is written: "The first man Adam became a living being"; the last Adam, a life-giving spirit.* (NIV 1Cor 15:45)

How does this sap flow into its branches? What are sacraments? Are they like simple tonics for the soul? Is our role merely partaking or something bigger? Sacraments are special arrangements for receiving God's grace and are administered by priests, whose anointing is through an unbroken apostolic succession handed down by Jesus. As we all know, Jesus chose apostles as per the Father's Will, gave them formation and consecrated them to continue His salvific ministry; Peter was appointed by Jesus to lead this ministry which is the Church. Pope Francis is the current incumbent of this divine office—Vicar of Christ.

I tried to explore and grasp how the **sacramental salvation process of the Church** operates and was amazed by the learning experience. Now, I have no doubt at all that by the aid of sacraments, it is possible to attain a lasting state of grace free from even residual sin (unrepented sins and unshed vices) in this life itself. In other words, through God's self-revelation in Jesus, the Way to God is brighter than ever before and we have **an extraordinary provision called Church to aspire attaining ultimate fitness in this life itself**. The gist of my experiences and some key learnings are shared here.

I had strayed into atheism even as a teenager and was growing from bad to worse. Though I was most fortunate to return to the Church after my marriage, it was quite a nonchalant comeback. Eleven years later an unusual encounter with God sent me into a state of deep pondering and taking a relook at my life.

Four months later, one Sunday as I started back from Church with family, my wife got this kind idea of saying 'hello' to the Parish Priest. I grumbled saying that coming to Church was burden enough and suggested we better stay away from the despicable tribe called priests. But she gently managed to have her way and the priest greeted us and took down our address. I warned my wife that we had invited unnecessary trouble for ourselves but she was unperturbed and calmed me easily. Fr. Jerome dropped in a few days later and presented me with a pocket-size red prayer book and left almost immediately.

Within a few days very strange changes happened: addiction to drinking and smoking left me abruptly for no effort of mine and I started going to Holy Mass daily. Thereafter, I was smoothly drawn into a close friendship with Jesus and never again craved for the company of friends like before as all restlessness vanished. Many more wonderful developments followed: tears, repentance, zealous efforts to amend self, a keen interest in the Bible and an understanding that impressed priests so much that they treat me like one of their own kind till this day.

Before my change of heart I did not know that I was proud and considered myself humble and modest. But after I started battling my sinfulness, it became very clear to me that my stumbling is mainly caused by pride. Out of pride, I once felt that a sinful priest is unfit to administer the **Sacrament of Reconciliation** and foolishly let the thought linger. Even as I was about to conclude that I was right, the idea to verify this experimentally came to me. I mustered courage to repeat the same confession to two different priests of whom I had formed opinions as good and bad. The outcome dumbfounded me, as I received verbatim identical wonderful counsels and experienced the same joy of absolution. I gladly shed my foolish doubt like a hot potato and that very moment, engraved it on my heart that God Himself acts through the priest.

I am aware of people who think it is just fine to confess all sins directly to God; somehow, this most common delusion that keeps many away from confession, spared me. One day a youngster confronted me with this question: "May we confess our sins directly to God instead of going through the priest?" and I was able to respond immediately only because God enabled me to say this: "God already knows all what we ever did and there is hardly any effort or humbling in confessing directly to God. But admitting our wrong doings to a fellow human is really difficult and requires real humbling and contriteness. Moreover, very few are able to hear God's voice and that is why He has anointed priests for this purpose from whom we may hear clearly and also receive God's own absolution and counsel".

Forgiving and repentance are conjoined twin graces; God offers these twin graces to one and all and my most precious learning is this: the sincere participation in the **Sacrament of Reconciliation** is a sure means to amend self, grow in love and untiringly sustain the war on sinful habits till they quit.

Unless we acknowledge that we are rotting and desire to become incorruptible, we will not be able to fathom the preciousness of the **Sacrament of Eucharist**. While the likes of David had to spend a lifetime in unceasing prayer (see Ps 51), we are offered the benefit on a platter and yet there are few takers. Many say: "Eucharist is just a ritual in remembrance of Jesus' supreme sacrifice and the bread and wine are not really His body and blood". Such ideas simply bounce off my head and it baffles me that people can think so, in spite of the painstaking discourse by our Lord exclusively on this subject (see John 6). His exhortations and the manner in which, many left Him even then out of unbelief, clearly suggest that it is the **litmus test of fundamental faith**.

Though we may not compare the different sacraments it is hard to deny that Eucharist is the main gamechanger and is literally **sap of the tree of life**. I have no doubt at all that my friendship with God grows through this sacrament and am amazed by the transforming power of the Eucharist. No wonder it is called goodness (நன்மை) in Tamil.

Overcoming the flesh becomes a reality when we sincerely partake of this sacrament. As vices start dying and virtues grow, one feels as if own self is waning to let Jesus actively indwell. Its power is not limited to enabling us overcome the flesh and the same grace continues to enable sustained perseverance for bearing good fruits in abundance. Total cleansing and abundant fruitfulness in this life itself, are the sweet rewards of patient and humble perseverance in faith (मेहनत का फल मीठा होता है). There was a time when I used to seethe with anger at the sight of anyone who had hurt me or was wicked in my opinion. But nowadays I am able to greet every known person with a cheerful smile and past hurts from betrayals and insults neither torment nor influence me like before. Foretastes of victory keep hopes alive but it would be premature and very risky to celebrate.

A worthy partaker in the Eucharistic celebration, is able to receive Jesus' incorruptible body and gradually shed own corruptible body completely in this life rather than face purgation in the afterlife. We are given the opportunity to complete the ultimate milestone in this life itself—die to self and live for Christ. Paul's joyful exclamation: "*I no longer live, but Christ lives in me*" (NIV Gal 2:20b), suggests that his corruptible body is steadily being replaced with the incorruptible body of Jesus and he is looking forward to being taken straight to Heaven by our Lord (see 2Tim 4:7-8).

Jesus has left us an extraordinary and most precious gift through which He continues to be with us physically and will be so till the end of times (see Mt 28:20). He could not have meant spiritual presence which was always there and will continue even after the end of times. By His stating this so clearly we are able to discern that it is indeed physical presence and NOT spiritual presence. The Ascended Lord's glorious spiritual body is reverse transfigured daily into flesh and blood and this is how the incarnate God with us, remains with us physically till the end of times, even after having ascended into His glory. It is miraculously accomplished by God and the power of His Holy Spirit transubstantiates the unleavened bread and wine consecrated by His anointed ones, into Jesus' flesh and blood. They are food and drink whose nourishment may reach only the souls of the faithful since the righteous are justified by faith and transformed thus into saviours in the likeness of Jesus. They become God's fit children and this is how God's real-presence in the world is actualized and truly manifested in all His children. The best way to understand it is from the testimonies of lepers and dying destitute who experienced God's love manifested through the likes of Mother Teresa.

Even the primitive believers of OT times could somewhat comprehend the term 'bread of angels' as the nourishment for human souls. But today, nearly half of Christendom lives in unbelief about Jesus' continuing physical real-presence. It is actually as simple as this: all of God's children are nourished by Him just like how a tree gives sap to all its branches. This nourishment is spiritual but the input is material as we are still trapped inside time and space.

The popular Indian saying—*marriages are made in heaven*, turned out to be absolutely true in my life. The **Sacrament of Matrimony** has been the greatest blessing in the lives of every member of my family. I have already described the key role played by my wife in my returning to God. Whenever I profusely thanked her for being the greatest blessing of my life, she responded with her conviction that all her values in life and even her understanding of God were molded and shaped by me.

Though we do not have a fixed routine for family prayers, we often joyfully gather together in prayer that could include praying the Rosary meditatively. We are prompt in pulling up each other for our wrongs and initiating repentance and can never remain at loggerheads for long, but invariably bury the hatchet latest by the end of day. Both of us consider it a sacred duty to instill Christian values in our children and have so far been successful without being forceful about it. All of us have noticed the hidden hand of God, guiding, preserving and blessing us often and are unanimous in our belief that being able to praise and thank God deep within, is the greatest charism and being quick to forgive and repent, is the greatest gift.

When my wife conceived the second time after 18 years, the gynecologist whom we consulted was a very nice but also 'matter of fact' person. She clearly explained the risks of child-bearing after the age of 40 and also the high probability of a deformed baby. It was God who led us to unhesitatingly go ahead and we told the doctor that we did not mind parenting a deformed baby but **terminating was no-way** and **unthinkable**. God blessed us with normal delivery of a healthy and cute girl baby.

The names of our two children symbolically mean peace and joy and we have learnt from experience that **marriage is a Christ-centered loving sacrifice that brings forth peace and joy**. In every town that we've lived (now the sixth) our neighbours invariably described us as 'made for each other'.

There is nothing unusual about either of us and in fact we come from very different cultures and are not very compatible. But our **highest common factor is Jesus** and we have never had two opinions about Him. Strangely, it was by clashing that we grew into tolerance and love.

I have heard (can't remember from whom) that the devil makes a last ditch bid at the hour of our death, to deceive us into forfeiting our soul and is also known to desperately try to overwhelm a person who is suffering from a prolonged sickness. **Anointing of the sick** (formerly known as **extreme unction**) is the sacrament which is instituted specially to renew trust and faith in God and give strength against losing heart due to prolonged sickness or in the face of death. I could notice the power of this sacrament in all cases that I came across and this is one amazing case: In 2002, my neighbour's only child, a lad of 15, developed a fever that did not respond to any medicine and so he had to be hospitalised. As his condition worsened, the parents, especially the father began to panic. I learnt that it had been diagnosed as rat-fever which had proved fatal in many cases and though the doctors were hopeful, they gave no assurance saying that cure depended on the virus being precisely identified through tests. When I visited the boy in the hospital, his father was in tears and very low in spirits and begged me to somehow bring the Parish Priest to anoint his son. He was also at a loss to understand why the priest had not come even after many days. That same afternoon as I approached the priest, he was the one to speak first, saying cheerfully: "I know that Adrian's son is very sick and I have not been to him till now. Tell him that I am coming this evening and assure him that the boy will be fine". I literally saw stars at his spontaneous response and can still remember that exact spot in the church compound. I was in for a bigger amazement; the boy recovered the same day and the hospital's recorded chart of the body temperature indicated that the recovery commenced at the very hour when the priest had spoken. (Recall Jesus' Capernaum miracle in John 4:46-54).

The scandals and schisms that rocked the Church throughout history and the current scenario too, are well known to me and I don't pretend to be unaware of the undeniable facts of history. But amidst all these disturbing happenings that target the image and credibility of our **clergy and religious**, we cannot be blind to the fact that our Church like Noah's Ark the Ship of Salvation, continues to stay afloat and lead us to our goal. Recall what our Lord taught: *"Do not judge and you will not be judged. Do not condemn, and you will not be condemned"* (NIV Lk 6:37ab). I have known both wonderful and scandalous characters in all walks of life and also indulged in slander, criticism, praising and glorifying. My experience taught me to refrain from either slandering or glorifying anyone, but gratefully remember the contributions of all especially the consecrated. The way God wooed me to conversion and the role played by a priest are my greatest experiential learning and the picture I have of the **clergy and religious** is that of **suffering servants**.

~ 9 ~

AIDS TO DIVINITY-II:
PRAYER & SAINTLY SUCCOUR

All the armours and weapons for battle will be of no use to us if we do not have the energy to fight. The only source of energy is **prayer** which is our life breath. The Holy Spirit inspires and directs the prayers of all those who love God and crave for Him. God Himself will teach us meditation, contemplation, introspection, examination of conscience and confession. *"It is written in the Prophets: 'They will all be taught by God.' Everyone who listens to the Father and learns from Him comes to me"* (NIV Jn 6:45). The Psalms are a living testimony of the kind of inspiration received by **the man after God's own heart**. However, not all of us are able to approach God with ease and a vast majority are still primitive in their state of development and education and find it difficult to even relate to God. Many are exploited by self-styled agents of God as they are too gullible. How does God reach out to these children who are as much His as any other? How to free the simple ones from unfounded fears and superstitions?

I was still unsure about praying to saints though I had benefited much from reading about the lives of saints. One day, while pondering on this, like a flash it became very clear to me that God leads and guides us in multiple ways so that everyone on earth is able to receive His light. He spoke through prophets, performed wondrous signs in Egypt, revealed the Law to Moses and finally became incarnate and showed us the Way to reach Him. While still incarnate, He said: "*While I am in the world, I am the light of the world*" (NIV Jn 9:5); later, while revealing that He was going to leave the world to re-enter eternity He promised: "*And I will ask the Father, and he will give you another Counselor to be with you forever—the Spirit of truth*" (NIV Jn 14:16-17a).

Now what about those who are led by the Spirit of Truth and walk in Jesus' Way? They are the ones of whom Jesus said: "*You are the light of the world. A city on a hill cannot be hidden. Neither do people light a lamp and put it under a bowl. Instead they put it on its stand, and it gives light to everyone in the house*" (NIV Mt 5:14-15). They become co-heirs with Jesus and His extended arms. His power is now as much theirs too. He delegates or shares His work with them and by doing so He reaches out to all shades of humans with their complex tastes, preferences and ability to relate with ease to a fellow human of their choice. He goes even beyond that by condescending to extend His appeal as the Infant Deity. Therefore, approaching God through His saints is very much a part of God's own plan. However, a true devotee of any saint or Infant Jesus is not a mercenary whose love is linked to favours and true devotion will never stagnate but grow in the right manner to blossom into discipleship. God seeks disciples NOT devotees.

These are the best of my personal experiences of saintly succour:

In 1999 we had for domestic help a respectable poor widow. One day she arrived for work in tears and narrated her sad plight—her hitherto loving landlord had suddenly turned heartless and ordered her to vacate the house by the month end. She wondered how he could change all of a sudden and was convinced that it was the devil's work. The demand of huge deposit money for renting an alternate place put her in a big fix. Sadly, I myself was going through a bad patch and her need was beyond my capacity to help; it was the only occasion when I lamented my economic state. That evening we prayed the Rosary meditatively and made a fervent plea to Maa Miriam to provide succour to Amna Khatoon. The next day, Amna arrived earlier than usual smiling all the way. She narrated what she claimed to be the most unusual miracle she had ever encountered: other than us she had spoken to none about her problem and swore that she had neither shared her woe nor sought any help in her neighbourhood. But to her surprise, the entire Mosque committee and her landlord were at her door that morning and her landlord announced loudly before the entire assembly that he would neither evict her nor raise the rent and that she could stay in the house as long as she wanted.

In 2008, there was much hype in my town about a miraculous spring in a nearby village called Nagamangalam. I was unimpressed and even made fun of some nuns who were planning to visit the place. A few months later an aunt of mine who lived in the neighbouring metro arrived suddenly on a Saturday, with her husband, son, daughter-in-law and grandchildren. They were actually headed for Nagamangalam and came to our place first as they did not know the route well and wanted me to show them the place. I accompanied them and we all visited the make shift church built in honour of Our Lady of Lourdes and offered prayers. They filled several bottles of the water from the spring which were duly blessed by the priest there and even gave me one bottle. I did not bother much about the water and the bottle just remained in my car.

Several months later, in the factory where I worked, a colleague of mine suddenly developed this strange psychological problem—an abnormal anxiety over his health. He was quite a sober and hilarious guy reputed for his efficiency and effectiveness in the shop floor. We were all quite surprised and shocked at his behavior and he seemed to suffer deep frustration with all the doctors he had consulted as they found nothing wrong with his health. With his persistent sorrow and anxiety he became an object of ridicule for his wife, children, relatives and colleagues. No one could convince him that he was absolutely fit and should simply stop worrying. After over a month of non-stop worrying and visible weight loss, he came to me and narrated his plight and told me that he was most hopeful that I would believe him and also refer him to a good doctor who could save his life. I advised him to see our company doctor who was due for his visit that week and also told him that he was the best doctor I knew. He promptly consulted the company doctor and was again told that his health was fine and he need not worry at all. He came back to me and literally broke down and said that he had placed high hopes in me but I too had let him down like the rest. At this, I did not know how to react and nervously suggested that he visit the popular Nagamangalam shrine which attracted people from all faiths. He readily agreed but insisted that I take him there as he had never been to a Christian church before. I promised to take him the following Saturday and he left satisfied.

That Saturday turned out to be unusually busy for me as meetings were scheduled for the whole day and were expected to go on till late evening; it was also raining quite heavily. When my troubled colleague met me at lunch and reminded me I pleaded with him to wait till the following Saturday. His face fell and he was very disappointed and accused me of not caring about him. I felt sorry for him but suddenly remembered the bottle of water lying in my car for months. I rushed to my car, brought it and offered it to him saying it was from that famous Nagamangalam spring. Even before I could add that it was quite old he grabbed it and gulped it. He turned perfectly normal that very instant and has never shown any signs of psychological problem till this day.

The year before last, my Parish Priest once called me over phone and told me to assist the nuns of a nearby convent who were struggling to help a hapless lady—she and her children were victims of brutality of their violent alcoholic husband and father. This priest was no great friend of mine and I was very hesitant initially. But I also felt that God was calling me through the priest and so I did as told, taking along with me another parishioner for support. The man and his wife were already there and all our efforts to put sense into the couple had no effect and the both simply traded charges against each other. Though the woman with her visible injuries appeared the more wronged, we took no sides. Finally one of the elderly nuns asked me to say a prayer. I recited the *Memorare* and then all of us came out, leaving the couple alone in the hall. After about five minutes, the two came out hand in hand and promised to lead a life of love and peace. A week later the man volunteered and went through a program for de-addiction and rehabilitation and thereafter they have been leading a normal life after over a decade of strife-torn, violent life.

Just a few months ago, I was returning with some members of my diocese after attending a state level seminar for diocesan representatives. As I stopped to drop my friends on the way at Dharmapuri, the priest in charge who had also accompanied us suggested I stay over for the night as the road from there to my place was notorious for highway-bandits, after dark.

While it was news for me I was also quite keen to get back home for supper and so politely declined the offer. After over an hour of driving when I was just 25 km away from home, all of a sudden two young men on a motorcycle overtook me and blocked my way demanding me to stop. I smelt trouble and managed to swerve past them and sped away at 100+ kmph, continually praying to Mother Mary. I heaved a sigh of relief as I approached a crowded hamlet called Aggondapalli and shed all my fears. To my horror I noticed on my mirror that the guys were closing in on me but this time I had the courage to stop. They too stopped beside my car and menacingly demanded me to get out. **What a miracle**!!! —even before I could make the slightest move for help, the villagers on the road grabbed the two guys who were after me and started thrashing them. They then respectfully told me to carry on and that they would themselves deal with those rogues.

~ 10 ~

AIDS TO DIVINITY-III: SUFFERING

Aversion for suffering and love for a comfortable and trouble-free life are quite natural. But even worldly wisdom tells us that lasting comfort is gained only through suffering. The unwarranted association of every suffering with retribution is the real cause of most of our mental agony. **'Why am I suffering for no fault of mine?'** is a very common complaint which we hear often. True, we do suffer many a time for no fault at all but how many of us realize and acknowledge the benefits of such suffering?

Remission of sins is insufficient to enter Heaven. To be able to indwell with God, our very tendency to sin has to be purged completely and then we've got to bear good fruits in abundance. Sufferings purge our vices and gain virtues. Salvific struggle is all about exchanging vices for virtues by enduring much suffering obediently. I have come to accept struggle as something absolutely essential for being transformed for good and share my understanding of the most painful and yet mystically joyful process.

Suffering is an indispensable aid to divinity. *If, indeed, there were anything better or more useful for man's salvation than suffering, Christ would have shown it by word and example.*

*But He clearly exhorts the disciples who follow Him and all who wish to follow Him to carry the cross, saying: "**If any man will come after Me, let him deny himself, and take up his cross daily, and follow Me**" (Lk 9:23). When, therefore, we have read and searched all that has been written, let this be the final conclusion – that "**through much suffering we must enter into the kingdom of God**". (Acts 14:22b) {IoC II:12}*

The above truth was already revealed through the prophets:

- *I will refine them like silver and test them like gold* (NIV Zech 13:9b).
- *He will sit as a refiner and purifier of silver* (NIV Mal 3:3a).

An anonymous author explains this parabolic analogy most beautifully: *There was a group of women in a Bible study on the book of Malachi. As they were studying chapter three they came across verse three which says, "**He will sit as a refiner and purifier of silver.**" This verse puzzled the women and they wondered what this statement meant about the character and nature of God. One of the women offered to find out about the process of refining silver and get back to the group at their next Bible study.*

That week the woman called up a silversmith and made an appointment to watch him at work. She didn't mention anything about the reason for her interest in silver beyond her curiosity about the process of refining silver. As she watched the silversmith, he held a piece of silver over the fire and let it heat up. He explained that, in refining silver, one needed to hold the silver in the middle of the fire where the flames were hottest so as to burn away all the impurities.

The woman thought about God holding us in such a hot spot - then she thought again about the verse, that He sits as a refiner and purifier of silver. She asked the silversmith if it was true that he had to sit there in front of the fire the whole time the silver was being refined. The man answered that yes, he not only had to sit there holding the silver, but he had to keep his eyes on the silver the entire time it was in the fire. For if the silver was left even a moment too long in the flames, it would be destroyed.

The woman was silent for a moment. Then she asked the silversmith, "How do you know when the silver is fully refined?" He smiled at her and answered, "Oh, that's the easy part—when I see my image reflected in it."

If today you are feeling the heat of the fire, remember that God has His eye on you and will keep His hand on you and watch over you until He sees His image in you.

Our merciful God offers the option of escaping if not minimizing the far more painful process of purgation in the afterlife, to all those who cheerfully endure suffering in this earthly life.

It is better to atone for sin now and to cut away vices than to keep them for purgation in the hereafter. In truth, we deceive ourselves by our ill-advised love of the flesh. The more we spare ourselves now and the more we satisfy the flesh, the harder will the reckoning be and the more we keep for the burning. (IoC I:24)

Our Lord's encouraging words: *"In this world you will have trouble; but take heart, I have overcome the world"* (NIV Jn 16:33cde), bring to mind all what He went through just to show us the way to the Father:

- humbled Himself to take human form,
- was born in a manger after being denied accommodation in an inn,
- patiently explained truth against all odds and worst opposition,
- re-assured the downcast only to be branded as 'a friend of sinners',
- endured calumny and most brutal persecution combined with insults,
- endured extreme public humiliation of stripping of garments and finally,
- died a criminal's death on the cross.

While all sufferings serve a **redemptive** purpose in general, they can be categorised according to specific purpose served. Thus, our Lord's sufferings can be described as **divinizing** and are borne for our sake and exactly define **Agape**.

The immediate consequence of sin is **retributive suffering** that serves as deterrent. I don't mean **karma theory** or the traditionally believed inescapable penalty called retribution, but the quick painful result of our wrongs that deters wrong-doing. It is not something that wreaks vengeance one fine day, but a hidden natural law at work which causes us to suffer whenever we sin.

The severe prolonged tribulation that frees us from the habit of sin is **justifying suffering** or **purgation**.

Adversity caused by the Enemy to dissuade us from doing good, is turned by God into benevolent **sanctifying suffering** that grows and perfects virtue. When we endure such adversity by the grace of God, we gain virtues which constitute divine nature. He beckons us to shed our fear for adversity saying:

Aids to Divinity-III: Suffering

"Come to me, all you who are weary and burdened, and I will give you rest. Take my yoke upon you and learn from me, for I am gentle and humble in heart, and you will find rest for your souls. For my yoke is easy and my burden is light" (NIV Mt 11:28-30). Some **sanctifying adversities** are hardship, servitude, failure, dishonour, ugliness, rebuke, humiliation, insult, rejection, persecution, blow, discomfort, trouble, pain, anguish and loss.

Glorifying suffering is the worst trauma that is endured during the ultimate trial—**Baptism by Fire.** It is the one which empowers us to say like our Lord *"It is finished"* before we give up our spirit.

Suffering in this world may appear heavy and unbearable, but God allows no more suffering than what we can bear. Our motivation to endure suffering comes from realising and accepting these twin 'carrot and stick' truths:

- the final glory that awaits those who abide and endure till the end and
- the unimaginably painful purgation process after death, reserved for those who evade suffering while on earth.

Jesus' titles include, **suffering servant** and **man of sorrows**; Mother Mary's titles include, **Our Lady of sorrows**. These testimonies of one of the tallest saints—holy apostle Paul, should encourage anyone:

"I have worked much harder, been in prison more frequently, been flogged more severely, and been exposed to death again and again. Five times I received from the Jews the forty lashes minus one. Three times I was beaten with rods, once I was pelted with stones, three times I was shipwrecked, I spent a night and a day

in the open sea, I have been constantly on the move. I have been in danger from rivers, in danger from bandits, in danger from my fellow Jews, in danger from Gentiles; in danger in the city, in danger in the country, in danger at sea; and in danger from false believers. I have laboured and toiled and have often gone without sleep; I have known hunger and thirst and have often gone without food; I have been cold and naked" (NIV 2Cor 11:23c-27).

"I consider that our present sufferings are not worth comparing with the glory that will be revealed in us" (NIV Rom 8:18).

"For I am already being poured out like a drink offering, and the time has come for my departure. I have fought the good fight, I have finished the race, I have kept the faith. Now there is in store for me the crown of righteousness, which the Lord, the righteous Judge, will award to me on that day—and not only to me, but also to all who have longed for his appearing" (NIV 2Tim 4:6-8).

May we design our own crosses? No, I'll never try doing that. True, voluntary suffering prepares us to accept and endure Godsend crosses; but it is best limited to token mortification prescribed by the Church. Also, the benevolence of suffering endured with grace DOES NOT imply that we simply watch people suffer saying: *let them suffer, it is good for them*. **Our sacred duty is to first of all reach out and alleviate our neighbour's suffering rather than give them sermons on the benefits of enduring it.**

Why fear in vain of death and pain? Thanks to the oral tradition of my land, I was able to see true meaning in suffering and thought it would be worthwhile sharing this ancient notion from Indian philosophy—**the created universe is a realistic illusion to segregate good and evil**. This can be compared to a **flight simulator** for training, testing and issuing a pilot-license where there is really neither aircraft nor airspace and yet people may learn and also be classified as fit and unfit, to fly an aircraft. Moreover **it is the safest way of training and testing as there can be no real injury or damage from accidents**. In this life too all creation came from nothing and is bound to simply vanish even as eternity remains beyond full comprehension; yet it is in this life that human beings come to know God, learn to walk in His Way and are segregated as fit and unfit for eternity.

This goes to explain the unbearable horrors of life that make us wonder why God allows them. **They've got to be illusions**, else why would He sit and simply watch? When He allows a horror to happen, He tests how we respond to it. In reality there is no damage done and it is truly **NDT** i.e., **non-destructive testing**. The story of *Harischandra* portrays it most beautifully and so does the book of Job. Our Lord clarified once: "*Or those eighteen who died when the tower in Siloam fell on them—do you think they were more guilty than all the others living in Jerusalem? I tell you, no! But unless you repent, you too will all perish.*" (NIV Lk 13:4-5). His teaching only suggests that what is seen and also felt on earth is no real damage but there is real damage in store only in the afterlife, for those who fail to heed the signs while on earth.

That earthly horrors cannot cause real damage is also made clear in the incident involving massacre of innocents: *This is what the Lord says: "A voice is heard in Ramah, mourning and great weeping, Rachel weeping for her children and refusing to be comforted, because they are no more." This is what the Lord says: "Restrain your voice from weeping and your eyes from tears, for your work will be rewarded," declares the Lord. "They will return from the land of the enemy. So there is hope for your future," declares the Lord. "Your children will return to their own land."* (NIV Jer 31:15-17)

To appreciate the efficacy of worldly trials and tribulations, consider the bombing of the Twin Towers. We saw both the worst and best of human behavior in this tragedy. Now, coming to the best, the supreme sacrifice of the American firefighters is permanently etched in my heart. It was truly a glorious death that will be celebrated by generations to come. Won't many try to emulate this sterling example?

Our heavenly Father is neither the author nor a spectator of horror on earth. Suffering is a consequential feeling whose painful effects are bound to vanish without trace. When endured by God's grace, it serves as a vital aid in realizing His plan for us apart from gaining great rewards in this life itself. *All our peace in this miserable life is found in humbly enduring suffering rather than in being free from it.* **He who knows best how to suffer will enjoy the greater peace, because he is the conqueror of himself, the master of the world, a friend of Christ, and an heir of heaven.** (IoC II:3)

Doubts about God's fairness and envy of the wicked are mere delusions that continually plague us, making us often wonder if we are struggling in vain: *"I was filled with envy of the proud when I saw how the wicked prosper. For them there are no pains; their bodies are sound and sleek. They do not share in human sorrows; they are not stricken like others. How useless to keep my heart pure and wash my hands in innocence, when I was stricken all day long, suffered punishment day after day."* (Ps 73:2b-5, 13-14)

The entire ordeal of Job—the blameless and upright, teaches us to shed all doubts about God's fairness and uproot even remote latent potential for this very sin - viz., questioning / evaluating / scrutinising God's actions and judgments. God is not culpable and hence above human judgment. All of

God's works are good by definition. To dare to question His judgments is sheer folly born of pride.

However, by seeking truth with humility and simplicity of heart, some saints have understood incomprehensible judgments of God: *"I strove to fathom this problem, too hard for my mind to understand, until I pierced the mysteries of God and understood what becomes of the wicked."* (Ps 73:16-17)

Our destination is heaven and life on earth is just a test to determine our fitness to live with God. By His own design, our earthly sojourn is but a passing phase of struggles. This is revealed when God gave Jacob the name Israel, which means 'struggle'. Worldly struggles are actually countless chances to err, learn and get fit by the aid of God's grace. Therefore, it is unwise to seek comfort in this life but truly wise to seek heaven without minding any amount of suffering on earth.

~ 11 ~

THE DIVINE VIRTUES

Faith, hope and selfless love (agape) are truly divine virtues and all human virtues are rooted in them. The secret of gaining and growing in these virtues lies in our genuine desire and constancy in yearning. God reveals in Jesus that we may merely cooperate with Him and can gain nothing of our own. All our efforts should be a humble seeking as Jesus taught and it is better to refrain from any kind of zealous pursuit. This chapter is about the insights I gained in my pursuit of these virtues.

FAITH & HOPE

How do we gain faith and then grow in faith? After gaining faith how to continue in hope when it involves waiting indefinitely for God's response. I delved through every book of the Bible and was richly rewarded to find my priceless pearl, revealed completely and most beautifully in the Gospel of Luke.

In his portrayal of the centurion's humility and that of Jesus' amazement at the faith of the centurion followed by generous praise (see Lk 7:1-10), Luke is actually revealing that faith is indeed the fruit of humility. **The key to faith is humility** and in the human context, **humility is the awareness and cheerful acceptance of our low estate** and **perfect humility is dual acknowledgement of the infinite greatness of God and**

our complete dependence on Him. Our low estate is the fact that we are God-dependent beings who neither merit any praise for our capabilities nor may complain about our deficiencies.

Humility gains and strengthens faith. Now what is **faith**? It is the **opposite of hard-heartedness** and best understood as **belief in truth by virtue of spiritual vision, even when there is no tangible evidence, but unaffected by deceptive illusions**. Spiritual vision enables us to recognize truth as well as see through Satan's deception and is gained through an assiduous process involving longsuffering, patience and humble prayer. **Faith** may have a modest beginning like a mustard seed, but **by humble endurance of suffering**, it grows gradually to become steadfast and unshakable in the face of worst trials and enables **waiting in hope even when the delay is indefinite**.

It took me a bit of research to establish the inter-relationship between faith, humility and patient suffering in hope and these are my learnings: In Luke 11, after teaching His disciples how to pray, our Lord continues to dwell on the subject in order to complete this vital teaching in its entirety. In an effort to draw them deeper into the subject, He opens this parable of a man who rushes to his friend at midnight, to borrow some bread to set before his unexpected guest. Our Lord's suggestions sound strange for a moment. Why does He say that 'friendship will not come to man's aid in an hour of need'? Why does He expect us to go on pestering till we get what we want? We will soon realise, that a parable could not have been more meticulous and precise than this. It presses us to chip away until we discover the most precious diamond. This is what I read of the whole thing:

- As no one would like to be disturbed at midnight, it is unlikely that the friend will oblige

- Expecting the friend to act favourably as a 'matter of right' indicates pride
- Pride is easily hurt and hence bound to fail.
- Persistent pleading comes from 'gravity of need' and indicates a humbled state.
- Humility endures and is sure to win.
- Prayer is for dire needs; this may be inferred from Proverb 30:8 for the meaning of 'daily bread' and what to pray for.
- Patience, perseverance, humility, contriteness and longsuffering are all foundations of prayer.
- Our faith in prayer grows as we experience the fruits.

This is one teaching that provoked me to revisit countless times. It brought back to mind all that our Lord spoke about 'faith' on various occasions. The thoughts of our Lord's frequent withdrawal into prayer convinced me that **prayer is our life-breath** and we need to learn all about it in totality. The comparison of faith to a mustard seed (see Lk 17:6), suggests that faith is something that grows gradually. What our Lord adds immediately (see Lk 17:7-10), reveals that humility, patience in prayer and faith are very much inter-related and we gain and grow in faith only through humility, which in turn is the fruit of patiently endured suffering.

To validate this, take a look at the life of the patriarch Abraham, father of faith. Is not the process so conspicuous in his life story? If that were not sufficient, consider the example of the persistent widow (see Lk 18) which our Lord gives for us to pray without losing heart, concluding with the words: *"However, when the Son of Man comes will He find faith on the earth?"* (NIV Lk 18:8b). The paramount value our Lord attaches to this teaching can be systematically deduced by following the teaching sequence together with the content:

Firstly He teaches us how to pray with a most beautiful and complete prayer: "*Our father ......*" (see Lk 11:2-4)

He then begins with the parable of the man who rushes at midnight to his friend for bread. (see Lk 11:5-8)

He urges us to ask, knock and seek and assures us that we will certainly receive. (see Lk 11:9-10)

He reinforces the teaching with three short parables on how, we who are evil respond when our own children ask us for worldly gifts. (see Lk 11:11-13)

He revisits the subject in the parable of the persistent widow. (see Lk 18:1-8)

Elsewhere, He affords us the golden opportunity of seeing His teaching come alive — when the gentile mother of a demon-possessed girl approaches Jesus, He tests her by saying: "*It is not right to take the children's bread and toss it to their dogs*" (NIV Mt 15:26b).

He deliberately does this in order to give a live demo of how humility and patient suffering produce steadfastness and faith: "*Yes it is, Lord*", she said. "*Even the dogs eat the crumbs that fall from their master's table.*" *Then Jesus said to her "Woman, you have great faith! Your request is granted*" (NIV Mt 15:27-28).

Always remember Jesus' formula for increasing faith: *So you also, when you have done everything you were told to do, should say, "We are unworthy servants; we have only done our duty*" (NIV Lk 17:10). These words from a common but lovely hymn should become our motto: **May the prayer of my heart always be—make me a servant, humble and meek**.

The best example of humility is the response of Mary to the announcement of angel Gabriel: *"I am the Lord's servant," Mary answered. "May it be to me as you have said." Then the angel left her.* (NIV Lk 1:38)

LOVE

When God revealed the Law through Moses (see Deu 5) He did not leave him clueless but also revealed how to fulfill the Law: ***Love the Lord your God with all your heart and with all your soul and with all your strength*** (NIV Deu 6:5). Law is a standard set for achieving through the means called love which is the provider of enabling grace. This love (agape) is an absolutely selfless variety of love by which we love God for God's sake and also love those in need as much as ourselves, again for His sake.

The Parable of the Good Samaritan is a story that our Lord chose in response to a law expert's query: *"And who is my neighbor?"* (NIV Lk 10:29b). It is one of the most powerful in terms of drawing complete rapt attention from listeners. He had probably waited for the right opportunity to deliver His greatest lesson—**the love command**, and when it came He did the best possible job of it. True to His own teaching He proved to be most prepared for doing His Father's work at any time. I consider this parable 'the jewel of the Good News' and these are some beautiful truths to which this parable opened my mind:

- We cannot pretend to love God whom we don't see; we can only love His ways, teachings and commands.
- The Levite and the Priest represent the people who claim to strictly keep the Law.
- They fail to fulfill the righteous requirements of the Law because they neglect the key—Love.

- The Samaritan represents those who broke the Law by indulging in idol worship and were excommunicated from Judaism.
- Despite breaking the Law, the Samaritan is able to fulfill its righteous requirements because he has Love.
- Anyone who is in need of our loving kindness is our neighbour.
- Loving our neighbour is identical to loving God, because the unseen God invariably reveals Himself in the form of a needy neighbour.
- The written code on tablet is mere letter and simply venerating it is not true worship and cannot fulfill any righteous requirement.
- Centuries before receiving the Law, we were taught by God to love our neighbour when He told Noah: *"I will demand an account of every man's life from his fellow men"*. (JB Gen 9:5c).
- Like the Samaritan: *"Share with God's people who are in need. Practice hospitality; offer your bodies as a living sacrifice, holy and pleasing to God—this is your true and proper worship"* (NIV Rom 12:13, 1bc).
- *'I tell you the truth, whatever you did for one of the least of my brothers, you did for me.'* (NIV Mt 25:40bcd)

It is important to know the difference between 'keeping the Law' and 'fulfilling the righteous requirements of the Law'. Consider a worldly example like 'Prevention of Terrorism Act' (POTA). Keeping this Law means not resorting to acts of terror for any reason. The penal provisions and law enforcement agencies may ensure that the law is kept. However, there is no provision to eliminate the root cause of terror—hatred. Fulfilling the righteous requirements is something much higher. It is the rooting out of all evil from our hearts by spreading **love**, so that there is nothing like terror. To kindle the fire of love in humans, God bent down from heaven and poured out His love on the brutally enslaved Israelites and expected them to listen to Him. Gratitude is reciprocal love with which we begin our relationship with God; it is an instinct displayed by every creature as a reciprocal response to the Creator's love and something entirely within their control. God has gifted humans as well as every creature the capacity to love and express gratitude; it is the most fundamental form of worship by which creatures and humans joyfully acknowledge their complete dependence on God who in turn multiplies their joy. It gradually blossoms into selfless love which is just like God's love.

If we took a walk at day-break we would actually see gratitude expressed by trees, flowers and birds. Even a stray dog wags its tail in gratitude for the slightest 'kind gesture' and demonstrates much more to its benefactor. **The key to selfless love is gratitude** and we are already enabled and just have to choose to be grateful and only then will we be able to love selflessly and also grow in all other virtues. *Gratitude is not only the greatest of virtues, but the parent of all the others.* (Marcus Tullius Cicero —106-43BC).

This promise which God made to Abraham: *"...; and all peoples on earth will be blessed through you"* (NIV Gen 12:3b), attains fulfilment ONLY in those who have love as no other virtue can make us a blessing to others. *In short, there are three things that last: faith, hope and love; and* **the greatest of these is love** (JB 1Cor 13:13). Mahatma Gandhi, Martin Luther King Jr., Salman Taseer and Kailash Satyarthi are all shining examples of selfless love. Thus, they are truly children of Abraham who remind us of John the Baptist's warning: *And do not think you can say to yourselves, 'We have Abraham as our father.' I tell you that out of these stones God can raise up children for Abraham*

(NIV Matt 3:9). Abraham's Call is as much ours and we are all called to be his true children who are:

- NEITHER fanatics in faith
- NOR prisoners of hope
- BUT shining examples of selfless love.

～ 12 ～

KEEEPING SATAN AT BAY

Satan's modus operandi is explained beautifully in Genesis 3. His freedom is limited to deceiving us into believing evil to be good and vice-versa. As part of his deception game he generates impressive illusions to make evil appear attractive and good appear repulsive. In this process, Satan's main weapon is our own flesh and our battle is the inner struggle between our spirit and our flesh.

My struggles to amend self, exposed devil's dirty tricks and taught me how to resist:

- If I let a temptation linger then I am bound to stumble.
- If I am in awe of righteousness the devil makes me a self-righteous imitator of him. Under an illusion of being a saint I become a habitual Accuser. Much stumbling, led me to frequently despise self and repent in dust and ashes.
- If I am obsessed with overcoming a particular weakness the devil is able to make me fall repeatedly; after I noticed this, I resorted to prayer, forgiving self and thinking less about that weakness and could make good progress.
- Irritants that are not serious temptations:
    o A favourite deceptive trick of the devil is causing an abnormal rage or a desperate urge to do

      something and by succumbing I make a clumsy
      fool of myself, to my own horrible embarrassment.

o   The devil is an expert at causing misunderstandings
    and fights among colleagues and also within the
    family.

It is not too difficult to deal with devil's irritants and he usually lies low for a while and tries again at an opportune moment. **Two golden rules**:

- never succumb to an abnormal urge especially rage and resist the urge by recalling how many times you were fooled in the past
- always remember that if you feel hurt then the devil gloats and if you refuse to feel hurt he groans and flees.

But irritation can also become unbearable and unmanageable at times. How do we face unbearable troubles? I found it hard to believe in the beginning, that the irritating **devil is highly allergic to Mary**. But now I have no doubt at all that he flees at the sight of Marian devotion. Recall what God foretold: "*I will put enmities between thee and the woman, and thy seed and her seed: she shall crush thy head, and thou shalt lie in wait for her heel*" (DRB Gen 3:15). Believe it or not—**the Rosary is a sure means for peace at home and workplace**.

'Sacramentals' are holy objects that have been blessed by anointed priests and include relics of saints, the crucifix, pictures, statues and medals. Instituted by the Church, they are the greatest boon to simple folk who are able to relate with ease and break-free from superstitions while being able to resist real troubles from the devil. By strengthening our faith they are effective in driving away evil spirits.

In acute cases, it is best to approach the Parish Priest and this is what I witnessed myself: Way back in 1971 when I was just a teen, our neighbour who was an elderly, quiet and lovable lady in her sixties, suddenly became demon possessed one day. It was a noisy and scary spectacle attracting many onlookers. Some could recognize unknown languages in those loud cries and the desperate family sought the help of one exorcist after another (an *ojha* and a *baba*) but it was all in vain as they left saying that the demon was a tough one. Finally the family approached us as a last resort and my dad told me to go and call our Parish Priest. He came most humbly on his bicycle and did as he claimed at the very outset—drove the demon out with a gentle prayer in less than five minutes.

Our Lord has already won for us the major part of our battle and gives us this assurance: "*I saw Satan fall like lightning from heaven. I have given you authority to trample on snakes and scorpions and to overcome all the power of the enemy; nothing will harm you*" (NIV Lk 10:18b, 19). With these words etched in our hearts, we can face our battle courageously and confidently, encouraged by many foretastes of victory all the way. *The God of peace will soon crush Satan under your feet* (NIV Rom 16:20a).

~ 13 ~

THE PERFECT WAY
OF OUR TRIUNE GOD

In my understanding, God's self-revelation to humans as three distinct persons is to enable perception and comprehension to the extent required in the created realm and His infinite Being is otherwise beyond our comprehension while on earth. Now coming to the mystery of three persons in one Godhead, I was amazed one day to receive inspiration like a brief flash revealing the Trinity's way as the perfect way and the model for our emulation. This happened on Trinity Sunday, 2007 while mulling over the homily during Holy Mass at Santhome Cathedral Basilica, Mylapore. It was an unusually joyful experience and I felt as though everything had become absolutely clear.

I searched the Bible vigorously to try and identify distinct patterns if any in the self-revelations of each person of the Blessed Trinity, starting with the premise (based on John 1:1-3) that the Word in the OT and the Son or Jesus in the NT, are identical.

I was amazed to very quickly discover the functional distinction of the three persons and even more amazed to notice a striking similarity between the **basic human way** of performing tasks and the functioning of the Trinity. The immediate bell that rang in my head—we bear His image and likeness. I also felt that it is something we have inherited from God and NOT the result of an evolution, designed and controlled by Him. This feeling stemmed from the fact that God's image and likeness are eternal and NOT evolved.

The Blessed Trinity is a mystery, but not the works of each Person which are clearly revealed in the Bible. He told us: *Seek, and you will find!* (NIV Mt 7:7b) and that is what I did beginning with God the Son, Jesus Christ who taught: *"I am the way and the truth and the life. No one comes to the Father except through me"* (NIV Jn 14:6bc). Here are the details of my search and findings.

God the Son

Consider these verses from John's Gospel:

In the beginning was the Word, and the Word was with God, and the Word was God. He was with God in the beginning. The Word became flesh and made his dwelling among us. We have seen his glory, the glory of the One and Only, who came from the Father full of grace and truth. (NIV Jn 1:1-2, 14)

And now, Father, glorify me in your presence with the glory I had with you before the world began. (NIV Jn 17:5)

It is plain and clear that God the Son always coexisted with God the Father and is Himself God and is also known as 'the Word'. Now our search moves to the OT to know more about the specific role or function of the Word, remembering that 'word' is also used in the literal sense mostly.

Look at these verses from which it clearly emerges that 'word' refers to God the Son especially from the expression *'see his word'*.

*After this, the **word of the Lord** came to Abram in a vision: "Do not be afraid, Abram. I am your shield, your very great reward."* (NIV Gen 15:1)

*The Lord continued to appear at Shiloh, and there he revealed himself to Samuel through his **word**.* (NIV 1Sam 3:21)

*He sent forth his **word** to heal them and saved their life from the grave.* (Ps 107:20)

*He sends his **word** to the earth and swiftly runs his command; he sends forth his **word** and it melts them: at the breath of his mouth the waters flow.* (Ps 147:15, 18)

*But which of them has stood in the council of the Lord to see or to hear his **word**? Who has listened and heard his **word**?* (NIV Jer 23:18)

Some repeated reading and pondering will enlighten us that God the Son displays God's awesome power by doing wonderful things and is often described as **the Word**.

When we continue the search and compare the many verses that describe the doings of the Word, a clear idea of the role of God the Son, emerges gradually.

Again, here are some verses from the OT and NT that speak for themselves:

"Here is my servant, whom I uphold, my chosen one in whom I delight; I will put my Spirit on him and he will bring justice to the nations." (NIV Is 42:1)

".. the word that goes from my mouth does not return to me empty, without carrying out my will ..." (JB Is 55:11bc)

Through him all things were made; without him nothing was made that has been made. He was in the world, and though the world was made through him, the world did not recognize him. (NIV Jn 1:3, 10)

"The Father loves the Son and has placed everything in his hands." (NIV Jn 3:35)

"The Father judges no one, but has entrusted all judgment to the Son, that all may honor the Son just as they honor the Father. He who does not honor the Son does not honor the Father, who sent him. And he has given him authority to judge because he is the Son of Man. By myself I can do nothing; I judge only as I hear, and my judgment is just, for I seek not to please myself but him who sent me." (NIV Jn 5:22-23, 27, 30)

Now we can say with confidence that God does everything through His Son who is the second person in the Blessed Trinity.

Our understanding is complete with the following verse that spells out the role of God the Son:

"My food," said Jesus, *"is to do the will of him who sent me and to finish His work."* (NIV Jn 4:34)

God the Son is the ruler of the universe which was created through Him and for Him; our King is our Saviour who establishes justice on earth.

The function of God the Son in the Blessed Trinity, is executing the Will of God the Father, be it creation, redemption or judgment.

God the Holy Spirit

To understand the role of the Holy Spirit in the Blessed Trinity, I took the same course as in the case of God the Son—searched the Bible with genuine quest.

The scriptures are full of knowledge to completely flood all our hearts and minds; let us seek the help of the Holy Spirit to understand His work, as we ponder over these verses:

Before ever a word is on my tongue you know it, O Lord, through and through. Too wonderful for me this knowledge, too high, beyond my reach. O where can I go from your Spirit, or where can I flee from your face? (Ps 139:4,6,7)

O search me, God, and know my heart. O test me and know my thoughts. (Ps 139:23)

Let your good spirit guide me in ways that are level and smooth. (Ps 143:10b)

Immediately Jesus knew in his spirit that this was what they were thinking in their hearts, and he said to them, "Why are you thinking these things?" (NIV Mk 2:8)

Whenever you are arrested and brought to trial, do not worry beforehand about what to say. Just say whatever is given you at that time, for it is not you speaking, but the Holy Spirit. (NIV Mk 13:11)

The angel answered, "The Holy Spirit will come upon you, and the power of the Most High will overshadow you. So the holy one to be born will be called the Son of God." (NIV Lk 1:35)

Jesus returned to Galilee in the power of the Spirit, and news about him spread through the whole countryside. (NIV Lk 4:14)

"I am going to send you what my Father has promised; but stay in the city until you have been clothed with power from on high." (NIV Lk 24:49)

"But when he, the Spirit of truth comes, he will guide you in all truth". (NIV Jn 16:13)

"Anyone who speaks a word against the Son of Man will be forgiven, but anyone who speaks against the Holy Spirit will not be forgiven, either in this age or in the age to come." (NIV Mt 12:32)

Then Peter said, "Ananias, how is it that Satan has so filled your heart that you have lied to the Holy Spirit and have kept for yourself some of the money you received for the land? You have not lied to men but to God." When Ananias heard this, he fell down and died. And great fear seized all who heard what had happened. (NIV Acts 5:3, 4d, 5)

We can understand from the above, that the Holy Spirit discerns truth and guides all. God's power too comes from the Holy Spirit.

The functions of the Holy Spirit are (i) counsel God and whoever God chooses, by discerning truth, exposing falsehood and convicting guilt and (ii) custodian of God's power conveying it to God and to whomever God chooses.

God the Father

Having understood the functions of the second and third persons in the Blessed Trinity, the function of God the Father the first person, becomes evident. This single verse completes our understanding: *"Are not two sparrows sold for a penny? Yet not one of them will fall to the ground apart from the will of your Father."* (خدا کی مرضی کی خلاف ایک پتہ بھی نہیں ہلتا) (NIV Mt 10:29)

The function of God the Father is to will righteousness and control everything for good. (وہی ہوتا ہے جو منظور خدا ہوتا ہے)

God is indivisibly ONE SUPREME SPIRITUAL BEING, Who exists in the uncreated realm called eternity. But to us humans who dwell inside the created realm called 'time and space', what is revealed as **a finite fathoming of His infinite nature** is this:

- The awesome power wielded by God including creation, wisdom, might, prowess, healing, knowing and exactly revealing truth without colouring —these are perceived by us as a distinct person called the Holy Spirit.
- God's perfection in deciding accurately or taking 'the right decision the first time every time' is what we perceive distinctly as the Father who wills rightly
- His incomparably selfless and passionate love, purity and emotions like joy, grief and displeasure* and the zealous commitment that accomplishes His own Will is perceived as a personification of Agape and humility or the obedient Son Whose 'food' is 'doing the Father's Will' even dying a criminal's death on the cross for the love of humans (*displeasure, as used here means **anger that subsides soon** unlike **anger that conceives hatred and lingers**).

The perfect way:

The functioning of the Blessed Trinity is the model of perfection; let us reinforce what we just discovered:

- God reveals Himself as three distinct persons performing distinct functions.
- God the Father wills based on truth, rightly the first time every time and controls everything for good.
- God the Holy Spirit is the custodian of God's power, discerning truth and conveying truth and power to the Father, the Son and also to others according to the Father's Will.
- God the Son obediently does (executes) the Father's Will be it creation, redemption or judgment, availing all necessary power from the Holy Spirit. He is the Father's Love personified and His Heart, Body and Right hand.

The imperfect way:

How do we perform our tasks? The simplest way to decipher any pattern in the way we do things is to split tasks into bits and look at them threadbare. For this, let us consider some typical tasks from our daily life:

- **Bake plum cakes** – buy dry fruits, flour, eggs, sugar, rum etc., in right proportion; cut dry fruits and soak in rum for 45 days; prepare cake mix; taste and fill moulds; bake in the oven; cool, pack and store.
- **Buy a house** – consult brokers or friends; search ads; advertise need and look up responses; visit and inspect houses for sale; negotiate sale; apply and avail loan; close the deal and register property.

Every task consists of several smaller tasks and they form a tree like network. Take a look at each task and recognise the common steps followed by all of us to perform any task, be it small or big. For example, to buy dry fruits, we need to know about the shops that sell them and the prevailing prices; we evaluate and decide which shop to buy from and then we go and buy it. Similarly we enquire and know about resourceful friends and brokers; after consulting some we decide on one and go ahead with the choice.

We can recognise the **basic human way** followed in every task performed—decide based on advice (information) and then implement decision. Every meaningful occupation is made up of tasks that involve **discerning**, **deciding** and then **doing**. The similarity to the Blessed Trinity is so evident and only goes to prove that we bear the image and likeness of God.

Now, despite being potential gods having God's own image and likeness, we do not function in harmony and are often at loggerheads with each other and also within ourselves. This is because of the distortion or defilement wrought by original sin. Recall our Lord's remark in Gethsemane: "*The spirit is willing, but the body* (heart) *is weak.*" (NIV Mt 26:41b)

Human mind wavers in taking the spirit's true counsel. This wavering comes from the heart's tendency to overrule spirit's counsel prompted by the senses. As a result:

- our wavering mind spurns truth supplied by the spirit to decide based on the senses. Our spirit cannot bear guilt and that is why the guilty conscience (spirit) pricks the mind. Recall the Tamil proverb "*குற்றமுள்ள நெஞ்சம் குறுகுறுக்கும்*" and also what Valluvar taught: "*தன்நெஞ் சறிவது பொய்யற்க பொய்த்தபின்*

83

தன்நெஞ்சே தன்னைச் சுடும்" (Kural:293) which means "*What our spirit knows is never untrue and when we are not truthful it is our spirit that torments us*".

- the disobedient heart has its way in doing own sensual whim rather than obeying the spiritual decision of the mind (மனம் போன போக்கில் போவது)

While we may lament our imperfection we must rejoice in the hope offered by God and bow in gratitude that we were considered worthy of knowing Jesus and being attracted to His ways and remember His loudest prayer to the Father: "*I pray also for those who will believe in me through their message, that all of them may be one, Father, just as you are in me and I am in you. May they also be in us so that the world may believe that you have sent me. I have given them the glory that you gave me, that they may be one as we are one— I in them and you in me—so that they may be brought to complete unity to let the world know that you sent me and have loved them even as you have loved me*". (NIV Jn 17:20b-23)

We know and believe that the Blessed Trinity is the model of perfection; we also know that our Lord gave us this command: "*Be perfect, therefore, as your heavenly Father is perfect*" (NIV Mt 5:48). Can we not approach perfection by orienting our **basic human way** towards the way the Blessed Trinity functions? The most striking feature that fills us with wonder and awe is that, ***the three agree as one*** (WEB 1Jn 5:8b). This describes everything that is necessary for perfection– love, humility, mutual trust, selflessness,..

Intra-personal perfection is the inner harmony of our faculties—mind, heart and spirit. (The term mind is used here to denote the faculty of reasoning and deciding. While many writers use this term in the same sense, philosophers use the terms mind and spirit synonymously to denote the same faculty). Intra-personal perfection has already been addressed in previous chapters; now a simple portrayal of the perfected individual, based on the glimpse just gained of the Blessed Trinity's unfathomable divine perfection and a fair idea of our own undeniable imperfection:

- A mind that does not waver or consult many advisors but fully trusts the spirit's counsel, whose decisions follow the supreme will of God and does not worry but fully trusts the heart's commitment
- A spirit that is led by the Spirit of Truth and hence incapable of deceit
- A mortified heart stripped of all sensual cravings, obediently doing what the mind decides; most dependable, steadfast in adversity, loves only goodness and always craving for the Author of goodness
- *The perfect victory is to triumph over self. For he who holds himself in such subjection that sensuality obeys reason and reason obeys Me in all matters, is truly his own conqueror and master of the world.* (IoC III:53)

Inter-personal perfection is social harmony amongst individuals or groups performing the functions: discerning, deciding and doing, for a common goal. It is a social responsibility and both (personal and social) can become a reality only by seeking, knowing and learning from our triune God. The stumbling blocks that make this elusive are **confusion** and **discord**, both wages of pride earned from the **Tower of Babel**. But there is hope of transformation by gazing at God's ways.

When our job is to **decide**, we have no business to doubt our authorised advisors and cultivate our own illicit sources; we should also trust and fully support those who implement our decisions. When our role is **giving advice**, it must be accurate, complete and honest; not coloured with our own views or distorted. If our duty is to **implement the decision** of our superior, it must be **done** obediently as instructed without being critical; we dare not usurp the advisor's role or do according to our own convenience or whim.

Discerning: Invariably we jump to an erroneous conclusion based on our exterior view. To see interiorly and provide trustworthy advice we must receive and be led by the Holy Spirit. How is this made possible? *"If you then, though you are evil, know how to give good gifts to your children, how much more will your Father in heaven give the Holy Spirit to those who ask Him!"* (NIV Lk 11:13)

Deciding: Perfect decisions are driven by righteous objectives and are based on truth. We decide imperfectly when we succumb to sinful urges. We are bound to be tempted every time to decide contrary to God's will; then how do we manage? Have we heard of St. Ignatius' method of election which exhorts us to sincerely seek God's influence to align our decision to His will?

What did our Lord teach us? *On reaching the place, he said to them, "Pray that you will not fall into temptation." He withdrew about a stone's throw beyond them, knelt down and prayed, "Father, if you are willing, take this cup from me, yet not my will, but yours be done."* (NIV Lk 22:40-42)

Doing: Our Lord did the Father's will with absolutely selfless love and sincerity: *"My food," said Jesus, "is to do the will of Him who sent me and to finish His work"* (NIV Jn 4:34).

Astonishingly, He told us that we can do greater things: *I tell you the truth, anyone who has faith in me will do what I have been doing. He will do even greater things than these, because I am going to the Father* (NIV Jn 14:12).

And how? *If you remain in me and my words remain in you, ask for whatever you wish, and it will be given you. I tell you the truth, my Father will give you whatever you ask in my name.* (NIV Jn 15:7, 16:23b)

~ 14 ~

Conclusion

I felt it would be apt to conclude this work with some final thoughts on **true worship** which is essentially the way to divinity, and on the **second coming of our Lord**.

TRUE WORSHIP

Veneration and adoration are the products of inculturation and contextualization. They are undoubtedly desirable, useful and essential to relate with strangers to the Good News as well as for keeping the faith alive through generations. But if we've understood it rightly, the practice caters to the culture, aspirations and mindset of the simple and nascent entrants to faith. At any point in time they are invariably the target audience for the Good News and obviously there is a need to speak the language they understand. However, it is also a pastoral responsibility not to allow spiritual stagnation but encourage the faithful to rise higher and learn to worship in spirit and truth. Sometimes, during festive Novenas it is really good to hear a priest remind the faithful that **God seeks disciples and NOT devotees**.

We should remember how the Israelites came to adore the glory of the Temple in Jerusalem and that it was ultimately razed to the ground by the Romans as foretold by Jesus. Today the Israelites are left with only the **Wailing Wall** in the place of the Temple, where they regularly wail in repentance.

The lessons of salvation history speak for themselves and when the faithful refused to learn from them, God came down personally to awaken and enlighten. Of the many beautiful truths He taught I found these two very relevant here:

They said to him, "John's disciples often fast and pray, and so do the disciples of the Pharisees, but yours go on eating and drinking." Jesus answered, "Can you make the friends of the bridegroom fast while he is with them? But the time will come when the bridegroom will be taken from them; in those days they will fast." He told them this parable: "No one tears a piece out of a new garment to patch an old one. If he does, he will have torn the new garment, and the patch from the new will not match the old. And no one pours new wine into old wineskins. If he does, the new wine will burst the skins, the wine will run out and the wineskins will be ruined. No, new wine must be poured into new wineskins. And no one after drinking old wine wants the new, for he says, 'The old is better'" (NIV Lk 5:33-39). I see this as a clear instruction NOT to let spiritual stagnation set in but continually re-invent pious practices to suit the changing times.

Jesus declared, "Believe me, woman, a time is coming when you will worship the Father neither on this mountain nor in Jerusalem. You Samaritans worship what you do not know; we worship what we do know, for salvation is from the Jews. Yet a time is coming and now has come when the true worshipers will worship the Father in spirit and truth, for they are the kind of worshippers the Father seeks. God is spirit, and his worshippers must worship in spirit and in truth" (NIV Jn 4:21-24). This suggests that true worship transcends both ignorant idol worship on the mountain by the Samaritans and worship by the Jews in the Temple with real knowledge of God. Jesus is candidly implying that NEITHER ignorant idol worship NOR outwardly worship with real knowledge of God are acceptable, but ONLY **worship in spirit and truth**. By not raking the issue of Samaritan idol worship, Jesus is suggesting that the extreme view of fundamentalists on idol worship is unwarranted and in God's view the so-called real worship is no better than idol worship as both fall short of His expectation. Elsewhere too Jesus would quote Isaiah to say: "*These people honor me with their lips, but their hearts are far from me*" (NIV Mt 15:8).

Paul further clarifies: "*Therefore, I urge you, brothers, in view of God's mercy, to offer your bodies as a living sacrifice, holy and pleasing to God—this is your true and proper worship.*" (NIV Rom 12:1). By describing true and proper worship as 'offering bodies (selves) as living sacrifices', Paul is clearly identifying it with selfless love (agape).

It is truly right to give thanks and praise to God always for His amazing power and glory; but the thing to be bowed to, is His Will and that which is to be adored, desired and imitated is His selfless love. Others may understand Church teaching as it suits them but this is my understanding: Church DOES NOT exhort us to imitate either the Father or the Holy Spirit but it does unceasingly exhort and teach us to imitate Christ Who is the image of the unseen God.

If you are still confused about it just check if you understand hero-worship, then true worship too, will become clear: a youth may praise and thank Michael Jackson for his awesome performance and also admit that he is incomparably the best; but hero-worship lies in imitating Michael Jackson's style and that's how his fans show their love and admiration for him.

God's style is the sacrificial, selfless love called Agape and He says: "*Whoever wants to be my disciple must deny themselves and take up their cross and follow me*" (NIV Mt 16:24b).

The Trinity is explicitly revealed only in the NT; how was it hidden till then? I revisited the Genesis account of the fall of Adam and Eve, and strangely saw as **continuing original sins** the **vanity of women** and **male chauvinism**. Some sincere searching and deducing gave me new insights. This is how I read the Genesis account of mankind's fall: Adam and Eve who lived in the created realm, must have seen God finitely as The Trinity before their fall. God the Father's command (or Will) was communicated to them by His Holy Spirit who told them that they could feast themselves on all the created blessings, which are symbolised by the fruits of various trees in Paradise. **The tree of life** and **the tree of knowledge of good and evil**, placed exclusively in the middle are very different from other trees; they symbolically represent God the Son and Satan respectively. The Serpent is apparently Satan's temptation personified, which wrought these perversions: Eve adored God's power and glory which was perverted into a desire to become like the Holy Spirit and Adam adored the commanding and decisive Father which was perverted into coveting that role for himself. If only they had adored and desired **Agape** to begin with, temptation would have failed and they would have rather eaten from **the tree of life** and become ever-living worthy children of God. Had they got it right the first time it would have perhaps been that way every time.

God chose to be incarnate on earth as the Son and not as the Father or the Holy Spirit and we can discern God's plan from this —it is to make us co-heirs with Jesus. His plan for us is realized in our becoming His worthy children or **obedient doers of His Will**. True worship lies in imitating Jesus, our role model Who defines the Way to Divinity as the Way of the Cross.

THE SECOND COMING

God's incarnation happened when the time was exactly ripe and the wake-up call had become vital. That we had reached the end times (eschaton) and salvation had assumed a 'now or never' vital dimension, may be inferred from this purely scientific report, prepared from a Greenpeace pamphlet: *The planet Earth is 4.6 billion years old. By defining a biological year as 100 million years, this mind boggling temporal history becomes finite and fathomable. Thus, talking in biological years:*

- *Mother Earth's age is 46 years;*
- *she began to bear flowers at the age of 42…..*
- *mammals arrived only 8 months ago…*
- *modern humans have been around for 4 hours.*
- *During the last hour, they discovered agriculture.*
- *The industrial revolution happened just a minute ago.*
- *During those 60 seconds of biological time, humankind*
  - o *has made a 'rubbish pit' of paradise and*
  - o *has multiplied its own numbers to plague proportions,*
  - o *caused extinction of 500 species of animals,*
  - o *ransacked the planet for fuels and*
  - o *now stands like a brutish infant,*
  - o *gloating over the meteoric rise,*
  - o *effectively destroying this oasis of life in the solar system.*

While we may lament the self-destructive course of our created temporal world we cannot deny or refuse to rejoice, over the steady transformation of carnal humans into divine beings. It is a process that has clearly and undeniably made unprecedented progress after God's intervention through His revelation in Jesus Christ. It is God's greatest ever self-revelation, as it is an incarnation with historic genealogy unlike all other self-revelations which are apparitions, visions and wondrous signs. In the process of showing us **the narrow way**, Jesus has thrown wide open the gates of His Father's Kingdom for all humans. By paying the heaviest price to show us the way He is only inviting us to follow His example of selfless love. The growth of God's Kingdom in the last two millennia can be directly traced to the spread of the message of love. Barbarian lands have been transformed to become some of the best places in the world in terms of holistic socio-economic development (measured as human development index).

God's intervention has also simultaneously caused the steady decline and near death of all evil, which though not yet dead is surely dying. Thanks to our Lord and Savior Jesus Christ, today social change is sweeping the world like never before and social awareness, outcry and activism against all kinds of social evils is growing.

Jesus has accomplished the righteous requirements of the Law and completed His Father's mightiest mega project in just three years. His tribe is continually increasing and the knowledge of the Son of Man is filling every nook and corner of the whole wide world. His Kingdom will never end. *For the Lord himself will come down from heaven, with a loud command, with the voice of the archangel and with the trumpet call of God, and the dead in Christ will rise first. After that, we who are still alive and are left will be caught up together with them in the clouds to meet the Lord in the air. **And so we will be with the Lord forever*** (NIV 1Thes 4:16-17).

It is not a call to eagerly await His second coming, but a proclamation of the Good News that all those who choose to follow Jesus in **the narrow way** may look forward to the ultimate reward of perfect union with God, which is what the second coming is all about.

Glory be to the Father and to the Son and to the Holy Spirit! In the beginning was all darkness and gradually Divine light was revealed. The Decalogue through Moses was a brilliant lamp and a milestone, but God with us in Jesus is the ultimate bright light and a watershed in human history. May we all become like Jesus when He comes again! Amen!

Appendix

The Way of the Cross

THE CRUCIFIED CHRIST by Blessed Fra Angelico,
an Early Italian Renaissance painter, (1395 – 1455).
(Converted to grayscale)

~ 1 ~

PROLOGUE

The traditional Stations of the Cross are portrayed here in the form of a dialogue between two siblings. The idea is a better diction that effectively conveys the deep meaning and significance of Jesus' passion and death that could move people and also beckon them to be transformed while showing them how it is made possible.

Chirag and his wife Deepa are a devout middle-class couple. They live inside the Lighthouse compound in the coastal town—Ramayapatnam (in Prakasam district of Andhra Pradesh state), where Chirag works as manager.

They have two children, a 19-year old son and a 17-year old daughter; Roshan is already in college pursuing BCom and Roshni is still in school studying plus-2 science stream.

One Lenten Friday, Roshan is home by afternoon itself and is busy cleaning his bike. Roshni arrives at 4-30 and spontaneously reminds Roshan that it is time to get ready to go for the **Way of the Cross** (**WoC**).

Roshan thanks her for the reminder and they get into serious conversation as they slowly walk to church which is just a few furlongs away.

~ 2 ~

GEARING UP

Roshan: **WoC** has often amazed me for many reasons: the meditations touch my soul; I find the church invariably full for this occasion and even get to see parishioners who are never seen otherwise; I see many weep in church and it leaves me pondering deeply.

Tell me Roshni, do you think there is something mysterious in it or is it just meant to remind us of our Lord's supreme sacrifice lest we forget?

Roshni: Good you raised this question Roshan; I've always wanted to share my thoughts with you and learn more about it deeply. Maybe God is present now with us and is going to lead us in unravelling the deep mysteries of **WoC**. I too, often felt that there is more to it than meets the eye. These are some thoughts that often come up in me: despite sincere repentance we are hardly able to stop committing the same sins; how does forgiveness help if we can't stop sinning?

Roshan: Exactly Roshni! I too experienced these very thoughts. Once while pondering on this I felt inspired to recall the Parable of the Prodigal Son and was able to see a clear connection between suffering and change of heart.

Roshni: Your'e very right Roshan; no wonder there is something called suffering to bring us to our senses. This is the clear message I now get from the Prodigal Son that suffering is truly a Godsend blessing that brought great joy finally. I get this clear picture now: forgiveness merely cancels our debt and we won't go to hell. But we may go to heaven only after we stop sinning.

Roshan: Wow! That was beautiful; how well God leads us to the truth in this simple parable. My confusion is already vanishing and I'm quite certain now that there is something called carnal urge in all of us which is the cause of all our problems. The effect of this is the sin we commit which is forgiven when we sincerely repent and our penalty is cancelled. But the cause remains; it is not something to be forgiven but has to be uprooted and that is exactly what suffering does.

Roshni: Hey! That makes one more thing clear to me right now: in choosing comfort and avoiding difficulties, we are actually postponing purgation for the afterlife. Do you know how terrible it is in Purgatory? The suffering there is unimaginable and many saints have described their visions; just read what the Venerable Louis of Granada has written: *"Never did the martyrs in their most terrible torments, never did malefactors, though subjected to all the cruelties which human malice could invent, endure sufferings equal to those of Purgatory. Let him, then, if he would avoid these dreadful punishments after death, begin from this time to amend his life."*(SG-25). I've often wondered if it would ever be possible to be purged of all sinfulness in this life itself as Venerable Louis taught and now I see a clear ray of hope through the Narrow Way of the Cross.

Roshan: It is now obvious that Jesus is showing us the Narrow Way that leads directly to the Father's home. This entails enduring suffering in this life by God's grace instead of keeping purgation for the afterlife. To convince us, God Himself came down and went through the worst pain and death so that we may see, believe and learn that **Jesus is the Way** to become divine in this life itself. Why keep anything for Purgatory when we know how terrible it is out there? The **Way of the Cross** is undoubtedly the **way to divinity**.

Roshni: How true Roshan? Jesus lived His teachings and **the talk He walked is our way to divinity**. Our Lord's passion and death make excellent spiritual sense to me now and brings to my mind what He spoke once: *For I tell you that unless your righteousness surpasses that of the Pharisees and the teachers of the law, you will certainly not enter the kingdom of heaven* (NIV Mt 5:20). I am now able to grasp the meaning of surpassing righteousness and also understand what these verses are telling us: *Thomas said to him, "Lord, we don't know where you are going, so how can we know the way?" Jesus answered, "I am the way and the truth and the life. No one comes to the Father except through me"* (NIV Jn 14:5-6).

Roshan: I see clearly, **God of the Pentateuch placing before us Life and Death, urging us to choose Life**. By taking upon Himself such agonising pain He is able to render attractive that which is most unattractive—pain and death. On the other hand, by exposing the true colour of evil, He is unmasking the deception that makes carnal urge attractive and renders it most repulsive. His message is simply perfect and draws us to be divinised while simultaneously exposing the repulsive brutality or the 'demonising way' to which sin leads. Come; let us try to clearly understand **Jesus—the Way to the Father**. This time let us meditate on each station and learn fully all what Jesus is teaching us through His sufferings.

~ 3 ~

THE STATIONS
OF THE CROSS

I – JESUS SERENELY RECEIVES HIS UNJUST CONDEMNATION TO DEATH ON THE CROSS ENDURING A BRUTAL PRELUDE

Roshni: *When he was accused by the chief priests and the elders, he gave no answer. Then Pilate asked him, "Don't you hear the testimony they are bringing against you?" But Jesus made no reply, not even to a single charge—to the great amazement of the governor. "Where do you come from?" he asked Jesus, but Jesus gave him no answer. "Do you refuse to speak to me?" Pilate said. "Don't you realize I have power either to free you or to crucify you?" Jesus answered, "You would have no power over me if it were not given to you from above".* (NIV Mt 27:12-14; John 19:9b-11ab)

Look Roshan, how serenely Jesus responded to such false accusations and grossly unjust demand for condemnation? Would we have remained cool despite the strength to hit back? Do we bear injustice only when we are helpless? I love you Jesus; I too must learn to avoid detesting and cursing within my heart when I am helpless against an unfair authority or a strong bully.

THE NARROW WAY

Roshan: Really Roshni, instead of allowing anger to get the better of us, we must learn to bravely assert our innocence without the slightest anger. Listen to this, it is most inspiring: *"If I said something wrong,"* Jesus replied, *"testify as to what is wrong. But if I spoke the truth, why did you strike me?"* (NIV Jn 18:23).

Roshni: When we refuse to be overwhelmed by self-love but bank solely on God's love this is how we will react: *Jesus commanded Peter, "Put your sword away! Shall I not drink the cup the Father has given me?"* (NIV Jn 18:11).

Roshan: If we trust in God, then we won't collapse even when cornered and will have both courage and love to try enlightening our oppressor: *"You are a king then!" said Pilate. Jesus answered, "You are right in saying I am a king. In fact, for this reason I was born, and for this I came into the world, to testify to the truth. Everyone on the side of truth listens to me."* (NIV Jn 18:37).

Roshni: That was some divinizing light; now let us also learn to shun and avoid the **demonizing darkness**. Hear this: *From then on Pilate tried to set Jesus free, but the Jews kept shouting, "If you let this man go, you are no friend of Caesar. Anyone who claims to be a king opposes Caesar." Finally Pilate handed him over to them to be crucified* (NIV Jn 19:12, 16). Pilate was faced with the risk of losing his job if he failed to placate those who were demanding Jesus' crucifixion. Love for the world can make us demons too. We are no different from Pilate, when without batting an eyelid we deny justice to many, either out of fear of losing our job or just for growing in our career. This happens rampantly in all institutions and organizations on the cowardly pretext of obediently following orders. The victims are none other than Jesus in disguise.

106

Roshan: Are we not also fundamentalist in our beliefs at times? If we don't change, then, like the Pharisees we too will one day respond like demons to the best example of love as you can see for yourself in this incident: *Going on from that place, he went into their synagogue, and a man with a shriveled hand was there. Looking for a reason to accuse Jesus, they asked him, "Is it lawful to heal on the Sabbath?" He said to them, "If any of you has a sheep and it falls into a pit on the Sabbath, will you not take hold of it and lift it out? How much more valuable is a man than a sheep! Therefore it is lawful to do good on the Sabbath." Then he said to the man, "Stretch out your hand." So he stretched it out and it was completely restored, just as sound as the other. But the Pharisees went out and plotted how they might kill Jesus.* (NIV Mt 12:9-14).

Roshni: Can't imagine what **demonizing darkness** does to humans that they can stoop as low as to entertain themselves with brutal perversion: *They stripped him and put a scarlet robe on him, and then twisted together a crown of thorns and set it on his head. They put a staff in his right hand and knelt in front of him and mocked him. "Hail, king of the Jews!" they said. They spit on him, and took the staff and struck him on the head again and again. After they had mocked him, they took off the robe and put his own clothes on him. Then they led him away to crucify him.* (NIV Mt 27:28-31).

Roshan: Roshni, do you recall how Jesus busted the Temple scam involving money-changing and sale of sacrificial birds and animals? The clerics were the biggest losers and after their corruption was exposed, they are proving to be far more dangerous than rulers and politicians. Shamelessly and brazenly, they dare to demand the most brutal death for the innocent whistleblower: *As soon as the chief priests and their officials saw him, they shouted, "Crucify! Crucify!"* (NIV Jn 19:6a).

Roshni: Idleness can deprave ordinary minds too; they really had no axe to grind, yet stooped as low as to prefer the acquittal of a murderer to that of someone whose only crime was 'claiming to be the Son of God': *With one voice they cried out, "Away with this man! Release Barabbas to us!" (Barabbas had been thrown into prison for an insurrection in the city, and for murder.)* (NIV Lk 23:18-19)

II – JESUS WALKS THE TALK BY TAKING UP HIS CROSS

Roshan: While Jesus ate and drank with them did any of the disciples realize the meaning of Truth? *Then Jesus said to his disciples, "Whoever wants to be my disciple must deny themselves and take up their cross and follow me."* (NIV Mt 16:24).

Roshni: But now the time had arrived for Jesus to practice what He had preached and He showed the whole world what is the Truth: *Carrying his own cross, he went out to the place of the Skull (which in Aramaic is called Golgotha)* (NIV Jn 19:17bc).

Roshan: Now I have no doubt at all and my beliefs are further reinforced. His only purpose was to show us the way and He did it for us to see, believe and do likewise, rather than venerating and adoring Him.

Roshni: Very true Roshan; there is a price for being raised and glorified. What is it? How could humans have ever understood it? All prophetic revelations gave just a vague idea of it. To make us understand clearly, God divested His glory and came down to be a human like us and showed us the way to glory.

The stairway to heaven is no bed of roses; if the Son of Man and the Immaculate Conception had to endure such pain and sorrow, how can there ever be an easier way for us sinners?

सजन रे झूठ मत बोलो,　तुम्हारे महल चौबारे,
खुदा के पास जाना है।　यही रह जाएंगे सारे।
न हाथी है ना घोड़ा है,　अकड़ किस बात कि प्यारे,
वहाँ पैदल ही जाना है!　ये सर फिर भी झुकाना है!

The meaning of this Raj Kapoor hit song from The Hindi film Teesri Kasam of 1963: *How can you deny this my friend, that our common destiny is God? You can't journey to Him like a king on an elephant or a horse; you may get there only on foot. Even your mansion with all its chambers, has to be left behind. So why remain stiff-necked my dear, when you've got to bow your head anyway?*

III – JESUS FALLS THE FIRST TIME

Roshan: What do you learn from Jesus' fall? Having already endured such agony just to tell what it takes to enter eternity, He is now letting us know at the cost of more agony, that the going would get tougher and preparing us in advance.

Roshni: Very true Roshan. He is telling all of us that we are bound to fall when we try to follow Him; we should not lose heart but rise again and persevere. He, Who endured all this just to show us the way, will certainly strengthen all those who choose to follow Him.

Roshan: I wonder how I would fare in this journey: Will I lose heart with a fall? Will I say "enough is enough" and compromise my commitment to follow Him? Jesus, my Lord! I beg for the grace to be able to shut my ears to the Seducer's suggestions and endeavour to rise again after every fall, by drawing strength from You alone!

IV –THE DIVINE MOTHER MEETS HER SUFFERING SON

Roshni:

- Will I say yes to God for a vocation of sorrow, to save the world?
- Will I remain serene and NOT wail and make a scene, when the sword of sorrow pierces my soul?

Yes Ma, I realize now that my devotion to you means nothing to God as long as I fail to be inspired to bear sorrows like you for the love of God.

Roshan:

- Do I know that the only thing Mary seeks is that I follow her Son?
- Is my devotion to my Divine Mother genuine?
    o Is it all only about decorated cars and colourful processions?
    o Does it mean attacking those who doubt her perpetual virginity or do not venerate her?
- Has it ever occurred to me that giving in to sensual cravings or being a fundamentalist, would one day make me a demon like those who brutalised Jesus in front of Mary?

Roshan & Roshni: Mother Mary, we beg for the grace to grow from devotees to disciples under your loving watch.

V – SIMON OF CYRENE IS FORCED TO HELP JESUS CARRY THE CROSS

Roshan: Tell me Roshni, are good works necessarily a matter of own free choice? Was not a great work thrust on Jonah? Do you know of the blessings bestowed on Simon of Cyrene and his family? They received the gift of faith.

Lord, let me be a 'simple Simon' first, doing the good works thrust on me, that I may one day become Your able instrument, like Mahatma Gandhi and Blessed Mother Teresa!

Roshni: Did you notice those soldiers Roshan? They were too proud of their position and refused to help the falling Jesus. This is how pride makes demons of humans.

I can't rest till I've shed all pride. I too am guilty of being conscious of my dignity when someone was in dire need. If I don't change I may become a demon one day and force a meek child to do what I could have done myself. It never occurred to me before, but now I realize that the vulnerable and meek ones are **God in disguise**.

VI – VERONICA GENTLY DRIES THE BLOOD-BATHED FACE OF JESUS WITH A CLOTH

Roshni: Just see her and tell me Roshan, aren't women, shining examples of God's loving kindness? Do people recognize the Veronica in every mother, sister, wife, daughter, maid and colleague? I have no doubt at all that it is Jesus who liberates women without the noise of words.

Roshan: I hang my head in shame Roshni. We men always find it very convenient to let women do all the dirty jobs?

Who does these jobs in all homes: cleaning vomit, washing baby-excreta?

Lord Jesus, I beg for the grace to rise to the occasion, whenever You send an opportunity to serve with love. Let me be a man who serves with love of a woman.

"Jonathan my brother; you were very dear to me. Your love for me was wonderful, more wonderful than that of women." (NIV 2Sam 1:26bcde)

VII – JESUS FALLS THE SECOND TIME

Roshni: Do you know Roshan? Jesus' body was His burden but our blessing. It was prepared just for saving us; hear this:

"Sacrifice and offering you did not desire, but a body you prepared for me; with burnt offerings and sin offerings you were not pleased. Then I said, 'Here I am—it is written about me in the scroll—I have come to do your will, my God.'" (NIV Heb 10:5b-7 quoting Septuagint, Ps 40:6-8)

Roshan: I can't deny this Roshni: I live in safety and comfort but am surrounded by misery. I am too eager to join pleasure parties but too reluctant to help in troubles. The story of the Good Samaritan has merely been 'good reading' to me. Lord Jesus, thank you for opening my eyes. My body too is for serving others; let me not mind its burden, be it sickness, pain or fatigue. Teach me Lord to annihilate myself like You and become a blessing to others.

VIII – JESUS ENLIGHTENS THE WOMEN OF JERUSALEM UNMINDFUL OF HIS OWN AGONY

Roshan: Listen Roshni:

Jesus turned and said to them, "Daughters of Jerusalem, do not weep for me; weep for yourselves and for your children. For the time will come when you will say, 'Blessed are the childless women, the wombs that never bore and the breasts that never nursed!' Then "'they will say to the mountains, "Fall on us!" and to the hills, "Cover us!"' For if people do these things when the tree is green, what will happen when it is dry?" (NIV Lk 23:28-31).

Did you hear what Jesus told those women, Roshni? Does it not apply to all of us who come here to weep for Jesus? Is that why He took upon this suffering? Even after this, does it not occur that worse agony is in store for all those who are neck deep in sin, like dry wood ready for burning?

What a strong indictment and warning: instead of weeping for Jesus we better repent and bring up our children in His way so that they escape the foretold horror reserved for the unrepentant.

Roshni: I am beginning to realise only now Roshan. Let me ask myself:

- Do I often lament the damage but neglect the cause?
- Do I think that my love for Jesus is greater than that of His serene mother?
- Do I try to impress others by wailing aloud over another's suffering?
- Can my loud wailing alleviate a victim's pain?

- Have I ever cared to seek and follow those ways that truly comfort my Lord?

IX – JESUS FALLS THE THIRD TIME

Roshan: This was prophesied long ago Roshni:

Do not leave me alone in my distress; come close, there is none else to help. Many bulls have surrounded me; fierce bulls of Bashan close me in. (Ps 22:12-13)

I wonder what went on in Jesus' mind? Did He also tell Himself: "Now, it is a perfect three—am I about to overcome the world? Is my Father coming to rescue me?"

Roshni: Could be true Roshan. I remember reading that God never tests anyone beyond His ability to endure.

Three signifies 'just right' and Jesus is reinforcing this truth and telling all of us that God never allows any more suffering than what one can bear. His purpose in sending suffering is to prosper us and not to harm us.

"For I know the plans I have for you," declares the Lord, "plans to prosper you and not to harm you, plans to give you hope and a future". (NIV Jer 29:11)

Surely it was for my benefit that I suffered such anguish. In your love you kept me from the pit of destruction. (NIV Is 38:17ab)

Hope in Him, hold firm and take heart. Hope in the Lord! (Ps 27:14)

X –JESUS BEARS THE WORST HUMILIATION OF PUBLIC STRIPPING

Roshni: Pride is called the **Root of Evil** that defiled human race. Our Lord's example urges us to shed our pride by enduring such humiliation. Were these His prayers?

- Father! Let my humiliation shatter human pride.
- May they realise the truth and be set free from pride.

Strive for this, pray for this, desire this—to be stripped of all selfishness and naked to follow the naked Jesus, to die to self and live forever for God. (IoC III:37)

Roshan: Let me introspect Roshni.

- Am I too concerned about my reputation among humans?
- How do I appear in God's view—clothed or naked?

You do not realize that you are wretched, pitiful, poor, blind and naked. (NIV Rev 3:17b)

XI –NAILS ARE DRIVEN THROUGH JESUS' HANDS & FEET

Roshni: This too was prophesied long ago Roshan:

They tear holes in my hands and my feet and lay me in the dust of death. (Ps 22:17b)

All carnal decay followed pride. After teaching us, how humiliation enables us to shed pride, our Lord goes on to endure more agony to teach us how to stem the rot called carnal decay by enduring physical pain. Mother Teresa once wrote: "—*the poverty of the poor must be often so hard for them. When I went round looking for a home, I walked and walked till my legs and arms ached. I thought how they must also ache in body and soul looking for home, food, help*". (Mother Teresa's Diary entry, Feb 6, 1949)

- Do I love luxury and comfort but avoid discomfort and pain?
- Do I prefer the path of least resistance to the rough mortifying way?

If the above answers are 'yes' then we may either look forward to unimaginably painful purgation in the afterlife or choose to change here and now by learning from Jesus and Mother Teresa.

Roshan: Read this carefully Roshni; do you notice something unusual?

Jesus said, "Father, forgive them, for they do not know what they are doing" (NIV Lk 23:34a)

Jesus chose NOT to exercise Divine authority to forgive, but humbly pleaded like a human who knew what lay in store for the enemy. Do you understand His message? He is telling us that spiritual vision alone makes it possible to foresee the peril in store for our enemies and spontaneously forgive and intercede for them. Recall how martyr Stephen could do likewise while being stoned to death.

By shedding pride and sensual cravings a fallen human regains spiritual vision and may foresee the terrible end that awaits enemies, which is going to be far more severe than the hurt they inflict. Without spiritual vision, how can we be moved with compassion for those who torment us?

Roshni: Amazingly true Roshan. I used to wonder how anyone could love beastly enemies and plead with God for them. Now I understand how it is possible.

XII –JESUS GOES THROUGH BAPTISM BY FIRE TO FINISH HIS WORK BEFORE GIVING UP HIS SPIRIT

Roshni: Tell me Roshan, what is this Baptism that Jesus is talking about?

"I have come to bring fire on the earth, and how I wish it were already kindled! But I have a baptism to undergo, and how distressed I am until it is completed! (NIV Lk 12:49-50)

Roshan: This is the Baptism that Jesus was talking about:

From the sixth hour until the ninth hour darkness came over all the land. About the ninth hour Jesus cried out in a loud voice, "My God, my God, why have you forsaken me?" (NIV Mt 27:45, 46ac or Mk 15:33-34ac)

Do we have any idea of the agony of being cut-off from God the Father, even if it is just three hours? **Baptism by Fire** is the ultimate kenosis or total self-annihilation. It can only be endured by a divine person. Jesus went through this most painful test, only to let us know that we too must pass this test to reach the Father and this is how our fitness for eternity is proved.

Roshni: What do these words mean? Are we all saved once and for all?

Jesus said, "It is finished." With that, he bowed his head and gave up His spirit. (NIV Jn 19:30bc)

Roshan: He has finished His part and now it is our turn to do our part. Jesus has certainly undone the imminent consequence of original sin and most firmly reinforced the hope of eternal life. He has fulfilled the Father's promise of salvation revealed in the Scriptures by showing all of us the Way to reach Heaven; but then, to get there we must walk in His Way. This truth is made absolutely clear in His life and teachings which was exactly His earthly mission.

Roshni: Do I know this? *Everyone will be salted with fire.* (NIV Mk 9:49)

Have I ever desired to break free from my sinful habits?

What is my preparedness? Will I withstand **Baptism by Fire**?

XIII – MARY RECEIVES THE BODY OF HER SLAIN SON

Roshni: What a divine being was Mary!

- Her apt description in God's words: *"Hail, full of grace!"* (DRB Lk 1:28c)
- Her true recognition by inspired children: Divine Mother
- Her fulfilled prophesy: *"From now on all generations will call me blessed."* (NIV Lk 1:48b)

- Am I critical of Marian devotion but at the same time, unable to follow Jesus' Way?
- Have I spurned the idea of Mary's help to follow Jesus?

Roshan: Let us pray:

Hail Mary, full of grace. The Lord is with you. Blessed are you among women, and blessed is the fruit of your womb, Jesus.

Holy Mary, Mother of God, pray for us sinners, now and at the hour of our death. Amen. (3)

XIV –JESUS IS BURIED IN ANOTHER'S TOMB

Roshni: What an example of simplicity and true poverty: Born in a manger, buried in another's tomb; His constant companion—poverty. My eyes are flooded Roshan.

Jesus my Lord! I too must love poverty. Change my heart Lord, lest I live and die in guilt.

Roshan: Are you experiencing the peace Roshni? Isn't it real? It is truly proof of a mission accomplished—a peace that surpasses human understanding. If prayer and meditation could give us this foretaste of heaven, then you can imagine how it would be if we really walked His way.

How can we stop at this? No, we must make His Way our own. Now I long for the grace to follow you Jesus and confess that:

- I've all along tried to buy my peace with worldly riches.
- I have not experienced true peace that is serene during adversity

- My peace cannot be shared with have-nots
- I have often petitioned You to remove suffering but hardly tried enduring it with love or knowing the Divine purpose.

~ 4 ~

EPILOGUE

Parish Priest: Hello Roshan and Roshni! I noticed that both of you were in your own world and now I see you radiant with grace. Did you experience something strange?

Roshan: Yes Father! It was wonderful and may take days to explain all what we learnt now in less than an hour.

Roshni: True Father. Never before have I had such an experience. We would love to share everything with you even if it takes weeks. First, let us sit and write down all the enlightening inspirations we received today.

Parish Priest: God bless you both in a very special way and may you be saviours to many in the image and likeness of Jesus.

Roshan & Roshni: Thank you very much Father and God bless you too.

Printed in the United States
By Bookmasters